CAMBRIDGE LIBRARY COLLECTION

Books of enduring scholarly value

British and Irish History, Seventeenth and Eighteenth Centuries

The books in this series focus on the British Isles in the early modern period, as interpreted by eighteenth- and nineteenth-century historians, and show the shift to 'scientific' historiography. Several of them are devoted exclusively to the history of Ireland, while others cover topics including economic history, foreign and colonial policy, agriculture and the industrial revolution. There are also works in political thought and social theory, which address subjects such as human rights, the role of women, and criminal justice.

The Rural Economy of Glocestershire

William Marshall (1745–1818), from farming stock, became a farmer and then estate manager and land agent after several years spent conducting business in the West Indies. A pioneer of scientific methods of farming, he published widely on best practice, and was also known for his geographical surveys of agriculture. This two-volume 1789 work covers the county of Gloucestershire, but also includes dairy management in north Wiltshire and the orchards and fruit products of Herefordshire. A hands-on reporter, Marshall stayed in the vale of Gloucester to learn the art of cheese-making, and then spent a year in various locations studying local farming practice. Volume 1 describes the rural economy of the area, with the different activities suited to the different geographical locations and soil types, giving information on the types of land tenure, crops and animals, and providing a list of 'provincialisms' which offer fascinating insights into the Gloucestershire dialect.

Cambridge University Press has long been a pioneer in the reissuing of out-of-print titles from its own backlist, producing digital reprints of books that are still sought after by scholars and students but could not be reprinted economically using traditional technology. The Cambridge Library Collection extends this activity to a wider range of books which are still of importance to researchers and professionals, either for the source material they contain, or as landmarks in the history of their academic discipline.

Drawing from the world-renowned collections in the Cambridge University Library and other partner libraries, and guided by the advice of experts in each subject area, Cambridge University Press is using state-of-the-art scanning machines in its own Printing House to capture the content of each book selected for inclusion. The files are processed to give a consistently clear, crisp image, and the books finished to the high quality standard for which the Press is recognised around the world. The latest print-on-demand technology ensures that the books will remain available indefinitely, and that orders for single or multiple copies can quickly be supplied.

The Cambridge Library Collection brings back to life books of enduring scholarly value (including out-of-copyright works originally issued by other publishers) across a wide range of disciplines in the humanities and social sciences and in science and technology.

The Rural Economy of Glocestershire

Including its Dairy, together with the Dairy Management of North Wiltshire, and the Management of Orchards and Fruit Liquor, in Herefordshire

VOLUME 1

WILLIAM MARSHALL

CAMBRIDGE
UNIVERSITY PRESS

CAMBRIDGE
UNIVERSITY PRESS

University Printing House, Cambridge, CB2 8BS, United Kingdom

Cambridge University Press is part of the University of Cambridge.
It furthers the University's mission by disseminating knowledge in the pursuit of education, learning and research at the highest international levels of excellence.

www.cambridge.org
Information on this title: www.cambridge.org/9781108078801

This edition first published 1789
This digitally printed version 2015

ISBN 978-1-108-07880-1 Paperback

THE

RURAL ECONOMY

OF

GLOCESTERSHIRE.

VOL I.

THE RURAL ECONOMY OF GLOCESTERSHIRE;

INCLUDING ITS

DAIRY:

TOGETHER WITH THE

DAIRY MANAGEMENT

OF

NORTH WILTSHIRE;

AND THE

MANAGEMENT

OF

ORCHARDS and FRUIT LIQUOR,

IN

HEREFORDSHIRE.

By Mr. MARSHALL.

IN TWO VOLUMES.
VOL. I.

GLOCESTER:
Printed by R. Raikes,
For G. Nicol, Pall-Mall, London.
M.DCC.LXXXIX.

ADVERTISEMENT.

BY MY PRACTICE in SURREY, I became acquainted with the AGRICULTURE of the *ſouthern* counties. By my reſidence in NORFOLK, that of the *eaſtern* quarter of the kingdom was rendered familiar. By paſſing in YORKSHIRE the early part of life, by viſiting it repeatedly, and finally reviewing it analytically, that of the *northern* quarter became ſtrongly impreſſed on my mind. But, when I left Yorkſhire, in 1783 *, I was as much unacquainted with the practice of the *weſtern* counties, as if I had been a ſtranger to the general ſubject.

Having, however, remarked, in the widely differing practices of the three diſtant

* See advertiſement to RURAL ECON. of YORKSHIRE.

diſtant countries I had ſeen, the various means of obtaining the ſame object, and the varying methods of conducting the ſame operation, I was deſirous to become acquainted with the practice of the fourth quarter.

I had other motives to it than curioſity. For though I had yet no hope of executing my plan on the broad baſis I have ſince entered upon, I nevertheleſs had my reaſons for wiſhing to be poſſeſſed of a general knowledge of the Rural Economy of the kingdom at large. Beſide, in Norfolk, I had made an eſſay in the art of manufacturing CHEESE, and was deſirous to become maſter of it. The management of FRUIT LIQUOR, too, was a ſubject, which, being no where elſe to be ſtudied, was of courſe a farther inducement to my viſiting the weſtern quarter.

GLOCESTERSHIRE I found to be the only individual county, which could furniſh me with the requiſite information. Therefore, in the wane of the

ſummer

ſummer of 1783, I came into this county; and, agreeably to the plan originally propoſed *, took up my reſidence in a farm houſe;—near the center of the vale of Glocester: where, and in the vale of Berkeley I remained, until I had exceeded my expectation, with reſpect to the manufacturing of cheeſe; and had obtained a general idea of the rural affairs of the diſtrict, adequate to the purpoſe I then had in view.

But my regiſter, in this caſe, as in that of Yorkſhire, was not ſufficiently finiſhed, for public inſpection. Nor was it, indeed, ſufficiently full to bear the title I wiſhed to give it. My obſervations had been confined to one ſeaſon of the year: whereas to gain a complete knowledge of the rural economy of an extent of country, it is proper that its ſeveral departments ſhould paſs under the eye in every ſeaſon.

 Therefore,

* See Rural Econ. of Norfolk. Addreſs, &c.

Therefore, in the beginning of April laſt, immediately on the publication of the RURAL ECONOMY OF YORKSHIRE, I returned, without loſs of time, into GLOCESTERSHIRE: where and in its neighbouring diſtricts, I have remained a further time of ſomewhat more than twelve months: a period which has been appropriated, ſolely, to the work which I am now offering to the public.

IN A PREFATORY ADDRESS, affixed to the RURAL ECONOMY OF NORFOLK, I endeavoured to explain the PLAN OF THE WORK I was then entering upon; and hoped that I had left no ground for miſapprehenſion. Indeed, it appeared, to my own mind, ſo ſimple and ſelfevident, as not to be eaſily miſunderſtood.

Neverthleſs, from a general OBJECTION which, I underſtand has been made againſt it, there is ſome reaſon to ſuſpect that I have fallen ſhort in my explanation.

explanation. The objection held out is —"that the ſame ſubjects are treated of in YORKSHIRE as in NORFOLK."

To anſwer this as an *objection* is impoſſible: for had it been put—"that *nearly* the ſame ſubjects are treated of in Yorkſhire as in Norfolk,"—the poſition would have been fully granted: as being perfectly conſonant with the principle on which the plan is raiſed. It is indeed, one of the beſt evidences that can be offered in its favor: inasmuch as it ſhows the PLAN OF THE REGISTER to be ſuch, as, in its full extent, to admit under the ſeveral heads, every idea relative to the ſubject: for, ſimilar as the heads really are, in the two ſpecimens already given, I found not, in either diſtrict, a fact belonging to the whole circle of rural affairs which would not have fallen aptly under them.

The OBJECTS and OPERATIONS of HUSBANDRY, are, in *number* and *ſpecies*, the

the *ſame*, or *nearly the ſame*, in every quarter of the kingdom. But the methods of obtaining the objects, and of performing the operations, are infinitely various. To catch the VARIATIONS, whenever they are ſufficiently marked, whether with excellency or defect, is one of the main objects of the part of the plan I am now executing. Another, to give practical deſcriptions of ſuch PARTICULAR OBJECTS and OPERATIONS, as are confined to particular diſtricts. And a third, to regiſter the EXCELLENCIES and DEFECTS, in the practice of each diſtrict, relative to every other department of RURAL ECONOMY.

By thus adducing in each ſtation (were it poſſible) every valuable idea it is poſſeſſed of on theſe ſubjects; and by arranging thoſe of different ſtations in regiſters formed on the ſame, or nearly the ſame plan; the different modes of conducting any particular branch of management may be referred to, and the

the ſeveral practices be compared. Conſequently, in the completion of the plan, may be ſeen the various practices of the kingdom, relating to any individual ſubject.

An art ſo extenſive, and in many things ſo abſtruſe, as that of AGRICULTURE, muſt remain in a ſtate of great imperfection, until the leading facts belonging to it, which are already known, be reduced to a ſtate of reference. To raiſe ſchemes of IMPROVEMENT, public or private, before this be effected, muſt be an act of improvidence ſimilar to that of ſetting about the ſtudy of chemiſtry, or any other branch of philoſophy, by experiment, without having previouſly become acquainted with the facts that are already aſcertained. A man, thus employed, might ſpend a lifetime of ingenuity, without bringing to light a ſingle fact, which was not intimately known before he began.

Such

Such is the LEADING PRINCIPLE, the MAIN OBJECT, the SUBSTANCE of the plan. But this, as other SUPERSTRUCTURES, requires a GROUNDWORK.—— Rural economics are founded in NATURE: much of the art depends upon climature, ſituation, ſoil, and a variety of natural circumſtances. Hence, not only a GEOGRAPHICAL DESCRIPTION, of the diſtrict under ſurvey, becomes requiſite; but the THREE KINGDOMS OF NATURE, ſo far as they are intimately connected with the ſubject, require to be examined and deſcribed, with SCIENTIFIC ACCURACY.

Nor are theſe the only requiſites. The work, before it be fit to meet the public eye, requires a degree of finiſh. It is neceſſary that every part ſhould be conſpicuous. The excellencies, not being ſufficiently evident, perhaps, to common obſervation, may require to be *relieved*; and the defects to be *brought out*, and ſhown in their naked deformity;

nity; that their impreſſions on the mind may be the ſtronger and more laſting.

Nor does the labour end here. In carrying on a work of this nature, the reflection will be voluntarily employed, in drawing PRACTICAL INFERENCES; and in FILLING UP DEFICIENCIES; not altogether, perhaps, with ſelfevident or theoretic ideas, ariſing out of the ſubject in hand; but with PRACTICAL KNOWLEDGE, collected incidentally, not in any particular diſtrict, but in every quarter of the kingdom, and which, being nowhere on record, might be loſt to the general deſign, if not laid up in this manner.*

If

* It may be proper to remark here, that, (through various motives) the rural economy of Yorkſhire contains a greater number of theſe FUGITIVE IDEAS, than either the Norfolk or the preſent volumes; which, nevertheleſs, have their reſpective ſhares. They are frequently thrown into the *didactic* form; as being the moſt conciſe, and the moſt *practical*.

If the ideas thus offered by the reflection, do not appear to the judgement sufficiently aſcertained, to become evidently uſeful in promoting the general intention of the work, they are, with other unaſcertained ideas, ariſing to the obſervation in the diſtrict immediately under ſurvey, either thrown out as HINTS, and inſerted with ſuch marks of *diffidence*, as cannot eaſily be miſunderſtood, for the uſe of thoſe who are in practice, and have leiſure to aſcertain them; or, are ENTIRELY REJECTED.

The rural economy of Yorkſhire, if duly examined, will be found to be executed on theſe principles. Thus,—— to ſpeak in reply to the *objection*, which has given riſe to theſe explanations,—— under ſuch heads, whether they include general operations, or ordinary objects of culture, as were amply treated of in Norfolk, DEVIATIONS only, whether they ariſe from cuſtom ſituation or ſoil, are brought forward. But, where a crop a crop, or an operation, not cultivated or performed in Norfolk, arifes, it becomes a *frefh* fubject; and an additional divifion or fubdivifion is, of courfe, opened for its reception; and every thing deemed ufeful, refpecting it, regiftered. Again, where a crop or an operation common to Norfolk, is not found in Yorkfhire, the head or compartment of the regifter, which received it in the former, is, of courfe, dropped in the later.

If, in the rural economy of Yorkfhire, I had defcribed the dibbling of wheat, for inftance, or the cultivation of buckweet; or, in the rural economy of Norfolk, the operation of planting potatoes with the plow, or the cultivation of the rape crop; or had even inftituted heads for thefe fubjects; I fhould, indeed, have rendered my work liable to objection.

But, becaufe I had defcribed the general management of foils and manures; and the general operations of fowing, weeding,

weeding, and harvefting; the cultivation of wheat and barley; and the management of cattle and fheep;——as practifed in Norfolk;—— were thefe fubjects to be paffed without notice, in defcribing the practice of Yorkfhire! Or, becaufe a writer, on geography, has defcribed the mountains and rivers of France, for inftance, is he, in giving a defcription of Spain, to pafs over the mountains and rivers unnoticed!

But ill founded as that objection (if it will bear the name) evidently is, the making of it implies a degree of diffatisfaction, or, if the word be applicable, a degree of difaffection toward the work; and I am defirous to render it, were it poffible, free from difapprobation.

Perhaps the objection arofe in mifapprehenfion. It may be conjectured, that my ftations are unlimited, and my volumes, of courfe, unnumbered; efpecially as fome infinuation of this nature

ture was, I underſtand, tacked to the objection.

Leſt, therefore, ſome of my readers, whoſe approbation I am deſirous of preſerving entire, ſhould have conceived the ſame idea, it becomes requiſite to aprize them, that, unleſs I make a reſurvey of the SOUTHERN COUNTIES (thereby completing the FIVE PRINCIPAL STATIONS I have been led to fix in) the rural economy of the MIDLAND COUNTIES (now preparing for the preſs) will cloſe my SURVEY OF PROVINCIAL PRACTICE.

The completion of my plan extends no farther than to SEVEN STATIONS: adding, to the five MORE CENTRAL, one in the MORE WESTERN counties, of Somerſet, Dorſet, and Devon, and another in the MORE NORTHERN provinces; including Northumberland, and the LOWLANDS OF SCOTLAND.

At preſent, however, there is little probability of the ſurvey being extended to the two latter ſtations: and no degree of certainty of its being continued to the ſouthern counties.

This in reply to VERBAL objections.

Under a deſire——a pardonable one I truſt——of freeing the work, as far as in the extenſiveneſs of its nature it is capable of being freed, from objections of every kind; I think it prudent to take notice, here, of ſome leſs general obſervations: made in a more liberal manner, by a different order of men, and through a different channel of communication, the LITERARY JOURNALS.

But, in doing this, I muſt neceſſarily place myſelf in a ſomewhat delicate ſituation. The flattering accounts, which have been there given of the work (in *one* inſtance flattering indeed!) may ſeem to preclude every ſpecies of reply; as I muſt, in making it, place an oppoſition of ſentiment where gratitude, only, may ſeem to have a right. But ſeeing the very handſome manner, in which the

remarks

remarks are conveyed, I may with ſafety conclude, they riſe from a liberal ſource; and that *vindication* will not be miſtaken for *controverſy*. There are, indeed, only two which require the form of reply. One of them relating to a part of the plan of the work, the other to my own character as a public writer.*

The firſt relates to the botannical catalogues of plants given in the rural economy of Yorkſhire. But the remark, in this caſe, ariſes evidently through an omiſſion, or rather a misjudgement of my own. The objection made is, that no *proportion* of the number or quantity which

* Some ſtrictures on the inſtance of the effect of whitening grounds ariſe, evidently, in miſconception: owing, probably, to a want of perſpicuity in the paſſage: no *concluſion* whatever was *intended* to be drawn.

And the *looſe hints* on curled topped potatoes, thrown together in a *note*, with (as I conceived) every mark of diffidence, which words and *printing* could give them, are not ſurely fair objects of criticiſm. *What motive* could induce ſo very able a pen to condeſcend to treat them as ſuch is to me altogether inexplicable.

which each ſpecies bears to the other being given, the information becomes, of courſe, vague and unſatisfactory.—— The two firſt liſts were cautiouſly guarded in this reſpect, by ſaying that the plants ſtood in them *agreeably to their degrees of prevalency:* an explanation, which I judged unneceſſary to be affixed to the other catalogues; from which the obſervations alluded to have evidently riſen. In the preſent volumes, I have been careful to guard each catalogue.

The other remark relates to river embankments. In ſpeaking of the marſhes or fens, which now lie in an unproductive ſtate, by the ſide of the river Derwent, I have, it ſeems, propoſed a method of draining, ſimilar to "directions given for the ſame purpoſe, in Anderſon's eſſays relating to agriculture and rural affairs, publiſhed about twelve years ago."

I am happy to find that I have fallen into the ſame train of thinking, upon any

any occaſion, with Dr. ANDERSON; and am ſingularly obliged to the ingenious writer who makes the obſervation: not only on account of the very handſome manner in which it is made; but becauſe it gives me a fair opportunity of explaining, ſtill farther, the execution of my plan.

The part, which I have hitherto been executing, is drawn from PROVINCIAL PRACTICE, and my OWN EXPERIENCE: Or, in other words, is an accumulation of facts ariſing in NATURE, and PRACTICE, or of reflections aptly reſulting from theſe facts.

Excepting one inſtance, that of INCLOSURES, I cannot call to my mind one deviation from this principle.* But that appeared to me a ſubject of ſo much importance, yet ſo little underſtood, that, ſeeing the fairneſs of the opportunity, and the materials I was in poſ-ſeſſion

* Unleſs the article ORCHARDS in theſe volumes may be deemed ſuch.

ſeſſion of, it would have been wrong to have let ſlip, unneceſſarily, one Seſſion of Parliament, before I laid the materials I was poſſeſſed of, in the beſt manner I was able, before the public.

In the inſtance under reply, there is ample proof of the principle, on which the work is conducted. I refer, from the paſſage itſelf, to an inſtance, in which the moſt material part of the practice I recommend is executed, on a large ſcale, by raiſing the water with draining engines, or marſh mills*. In the ſame volume, only a few pages from the paſſage, I give another inſtance, on a ſmaller ſcale, in which the water is got rid of, by ſinking a counter ditch, only, without the help either of mill or floodgate†. And I knew, at the ſame time, that the Severn is embanked, and its meadows kept dry, by floodgates, only: and moreover knew that, in this caſe, the

* See NORF: ECON: min: 118.

† See YORK: ECON: vol. i. p. 248.

the banks being placed at ſome diſtance from the river, their requiſite height for the purpoſe intended, is rendered inconſiderable ‡: and farther, that, between the Severn and its banks, ozier beds are frequent; and ſhoot, in general, with uncommon luxuriance*. Poſſeſſed of theſe, and numerous other facts belonging to the ſubject, I had no need of books to aſſiſt me in drawing the *ſketch*, which is the ſubject, of this reply; and which I drew in Yorkſhire, becauſe I knew no inſtance in the other diſtricts I had viſited, in which the practice was ſo applicable, or where the art of draining in difficult caſes is leſs underſtood.

Groundleſs, however, as the remark replied to moſt aſſuredly is, I repeat my acknowledgements to the writer who brought it forward. Other readers, equally

‡ See this volume p. 12. note.

* See PLANTING and ORN: GARD: (publiſhed in 1785) p. 547.

equally unacquainted of courſe with the ſources of my information, may have ſeen the paſſage alluded to in the ſame point of view. Beſide, it affords me an opportunity, which otherwiſe I might not have had, of ſaying ſtill farther, that, from the commencement of the minutes of agriculture, in 1774, to the preſent time, I have read nothing on the ſubject of rural affairs; excepting ſome few modern publications, which have fallen caſually under my eye*; and excepting that, in the year 1780, I ſpent ſome weeks, or months, in the reading room of the Britiſh Muſeum, looking over and forming a catalogue of books, formerly written on the ſubject.

This

* And, among the reſt, a book written by Mr. Anderſon; but whether it contained obſervations on river embankments, I have not the ſmalleſt recollection. At the time I read it, river embankment was a ſubject totally unintereſting to me; and, ſuppoſing that I attended to the article, it is not probable, that any trace of it ſhould remain on the mind ten or twelve years.

This disregard of modern books has not, of late years at least, risen altogether through *neglect*. I have *designedly* refrained from them; *lest* I might catch ideas, imperceptibly,—and, by interweaving those of BOOKS with those of PROVINCIAL PRACTICE, blend the two parts of the general work, which I wish to keep perfectly distinct. And I have refrained more particularly from modern books, which have gained a degree of popularity; lest I should be led, imperceptibly, into controversies, public or *private*, which might swerve me from my main design.

The part of the plan which I have, hitherto, been executing has, in itself, been sufficient to engage every hour of my attention. I have purposely shut my eyes to every object not immediately connected with it; under a conviction, that the magnitude of the subject is more than sufficient for any man's attention; and, of course, that whatever part of it ſhould be applied to other objects would be loſt to the main purſuit.

My ſources of information are ample; almoſt without limitation. The two wide fields of NATURE and SCIENCE, ſo far as they are connected with the ſubject under inveſtigation; the ESTABLISHED PRACTICE of the KINGDOM at large, with reſpect to the three grand branches of RURAL ECONOMICS; the individual practice, and ſometimes the individual opinion, of the SUPERIOR CLASS of PROFESSIONAL MEN; together with intereſting incidents ariſing in my OWN PRACTICE, have, hitherto, been the objects of my attention.

CONTENTS

TO THE

FIRST VOLUME.

THE

THE

RURAL ECONOMY

OF

GLOCESTERSHIRE, &c.

COUNTRIES are characterized by rivers. Mountains are cleft to give vent to their various sources. Or we may say, and perhaps more philosophically,---rivers receive their general character from countries. In whatever light we view them, it is sufficiently evident that, in most instances, they are strongly characteristic of each other. The fissures uniting form a valley; the united rills the branch of a river. The mountains bow as the fiſſures widen; and as the hills ſink the vallies expand: at length uniting in one open vale; in whoſe lap the concurring branches form an accompanying river: which as it approaches the ſea, widens into an eſtuary; whoſe immediate banks are marſhes.

But rivers, as all nature's productions, are infinitely various. Each has its differential character.

The HUMBER (the firſt of Britiſh rivers) opens from the ſea with an eſtuary diſproportionately ſmall. But its banks ſpread wide; in due proportion to the vaſtneſs of the vale, in which its numerous branches are collected,---and to the magnificence of the mountains and vallies, which give birth to them. The characteriſtic of the Humber and its accompaniments (its eſtuary apart) is *greatneſs*.

The SEVERN is marked by widely differing characters. Its eſtuary is ſingularly magnificent; forming a CHANNEL; not unfrequently, nor improperly, ſtyled the SEVERN-SEA; whoſe banks, on either ſide, riſe from the richeſt marſhes to lofty and moſt pictureſque mountains. Europe, I believe, does not furniſh

niſh another River-entrance of equal grandeur.

Theſe mountain banks approach; and the *channel* contracts with the clifts of Chepſtow and Auſt; but the *eſtuary* continues; and the country, above, opens into an extended vale, which widens as its length increaſes; until it receive the county of Worceſter, almoſt entirely, within its outline: then contracts, and cloſes with the hills of Shropſhire and Staffordſhire. A vale, which in *richneſs* and *beauty*, has no where, perhaps, its equal.

Its banks, to the Weſt, are formed by the foreſt of Dean, Mayhill, the Malvern hills, and the hills of Herefordſhire, and Shropſhire: to the Eaſt, by the Stroudwater and the Cotſwold hills, and by riſing grounds on the border of Warwickſhire; cloſing with the Lickey and the Clent hills.

By hillocks ſcattered on the area of this expanſe, its entireneſs is not evident: Bredon hill, with ſome ſmaller hillocks ſtrewed at the point of the Cleeve hill (a promontory of the Cotſwolds) croſs the view, and partially divide the vale into three diſtricts: Worceſterſhire; the vales of Glocesterſhire; and the vale of Evesham, which is shared in a singular manner between the two counties. But remove these hills, and the hillocks near Glocester,---the whole forms one continued unbroken vale, which accompanies the Severn from the union of its principal branches to its conflux with the Sea.

Probably, however, not having been seen in this light, it has had no general name assigned it. The vale of Evesham lays claim to some part of it; but to how much, has not, I believe, ever been settled. Were it necessary to assign it a general name,--TEWKSBURY, which is situated every way in its center, might well claim the honor of giving it.

The upper part of this vale, (its uppermost extremity excepted) though abundant in *riches* is not *picturesque.* The idea of flatness is too predominant: its banks are comparatively tame; and its surface, though sufficiently broken, for the uses of RURAL ECONOMY; is too uniform to give full effect to RURAL ORNAMENT.

Passing downward, its more finished scenery commences with the Malvern hills: from whence to the rocks of Chepstow, its area and its

its banks form one continuous ſcene of pictura-ble beauty. A garden forty miles in extent. A grand ſuite of ornamental grounds, in na-ture's beſt ſtyle. Every part is pleaſing. The banks bold; and happily varied; and partially hung with wood. The area ſtrewed with hil-locks, *fertile to the ſummits*, affording endleſs points of view; while the hillocks themſelves are, in their turns, the cauſe of infinite beauty. The ſoil every where rich; and moſtly in a ſtate of graſs. The Severn winding with unuſual freedom. With the Welchmountains riſing in happy diſtance. Theſe features well aſſoci-ated give this paſſage of country a preference, in *beauty*, to every other this iſland is poſſeſſed of; and, in much probability, to every other this planet is adorned with. There may be na-tural ſituations equal to it: but where ſhall we find ſeaſons ſo favourable to rural ornament as in this iſland; and, in ſuch a climature, cultivation ſo highly raiſed?

Gloceſterſhire might well be ſtyled the ſeat of pictureſque beauty. It is equally a ſubject of ſtudy for the painter and the rural ornamen-taliſt; not in the outline only, but in the detail: the Stroudwater hills, and the banks of the Wye, are full of ſecluded beauty.

It is this lower extremity of the Severn-vale which falls within the diſtrict I have choſen for my preſent STATION. Not on account of its *picturesque beauty*; but by reaſon of its *ſituation* with reſpect to the other ſtations I have fixed in; ---its *richneſs*; and the various *productions* it affords. Had it not been *ſingularly* characterized by natural ornament, I ſhould not have detained the reader a moment on ſo *unprofitable* a ſubject. But the eye muſt be dim, and the heart benumbed, which can be inſenſible to the rural beauty of Glouceſterſhire.

The popular diviſions of the COUNTY are the *Vale*,---the *Cotſwold hills*---the *Stroudwater hills*---the country about Briſtol---*Berkley Hundred*---*Wye-ſide*---the *Foreſt of Dean*--and *Over-Severn:* the laſt a diſtrict, which, though it be divided only by the river from what is properly underſtood by the *Vale*, differs from it very much in ſoil and management; both of which partake of thoſe of Herefordſhire. The Foreſt of Dean a mere waſte, which calls loudly for improvement, and the Wyeſide little more than the banks of the river.

Among

Among the eaſtern diviſions we muſt therefore look for proper ſubjects of ſtudy for RURAL INFORMATION: and we find three of them entitled to notice. The vales of GLOCESTER and EVESHAM, as a rich vale diſtrict, equally abundant in graſs and corn. The COTSWOLD HILLS, as an upland arable diſtrict. And the vale of BERKLEY as a graſsland dairy country.

The *Stroudwater hills* partake of the Cotſwolds and the vale jointly.--A lovely plot of country: but not a proper ſubject of rural ſtudy; as being a ſeat of manufacture. The Southern extremity is various in ſoil and ſurface. The *Briſtol Quarter* is a fine tract of country; but lies too near a populous town to be ſtudied for general information. The *Southwolds*, a ridge of hill which joins the Stroudwater to the Lanſdown hills,---is in ſoil, ſituation, and management, ſimilar to the Cotſwolds: the Stroudwater hills lying in a dip between them.

The vales of Gloceſter and Eveſham
The Cotſwold hills, and
The vale of Berkley; as well as
North-Wiltſhire, and
Herefordſhire; will be ſeparately deſcribed.

THE VALES OF GLOCESTER and EVESHAM.

THE VALE which accompanies the Severn, through GLOCESTERSHIRE, has a natural inſection, which divides it into two diſtricts, very different in produce and rural management. Theſe diſtricts, in diſtinction, I ſhall call the *upper* and the *lower* vale; or the the VALE OF GLOCESTER, and the VALE OF BERKLEY.

The upper vale, in whole, or in part, is ſometimes ſpoken of as belonging to the VALE OF EVESHAM;---at preſent an *imaginary* diſtrict, of which no two men have the ſame idea. Some include, not only the vale of Gloceſter, but a principal part of Worceſterſhire within its limits! Its *natural* limits, however, are evident;

evident; and appear, from old maps, to have been formerly the received boundaries.

The VALE OF EVESHAM belongs to the AVON; as the vales of Glocefter and Berkley do to the Severn: being included between the river and the Cotfwold hills: expanding fouthward to Campden and Morton; and following the Avon eaftward to Stratford: Evefham being fituated near the midway between its extremities: that is, near the center of the VALE OF AVON; at the fartheft outfkirts of the VALE OF SEVERN.

The town of Evefham ftands in Worcefterfhire; but much of the vale lies within the boundaries of Glocefterfhire; and, in point of fituation, climature, furface, foil, produce, and management, may be confidered as a continuation of the vale of Glocefter. The fouthern part of Worcefterfhire, likewife enjoys a fimilar fituation and foil, and is fubjected to a fimilar management. Therefore, in the rural Economy of the VALE OF GLOCESTER we fhall gain a general idea of that of a moft fertile and extenfive diftrict: one of the richeft rural gardens the ifland has to boaft of.

The

THE VALE OF GLOCESTER

Is, in OUTLINE, ſomewhat ſemicircular: the Severn the chord the environing hills the arch: the towns of Glocester, Tewkſbury, and Cheltenham forming a triangle withinits area. Its EXTENT, from the foot of Matſon hill to that of Bredon hill (its *outmoſt* limit to the north) is about fifteen miles: from the Severn to the foot of Dowdeſwell hill, ſeven or eight miles. The entire diſtrict, therefore, does not contain a hundred ſquare miles. It may be eſtimated at fifty to ſixty thouſand acres.

The CLIMATURE of this diſtrict, like that of the vale of Pickering, is *above* its natural latitude, (51.° 55.') The ſeaſons on this ſide of the Severn are a week or ten days later than on the oppoſite banks: owing, probably, to the ſame cauſe, as that which has been aſſigned for a ſimilar effect in the vale abovementioned. The Cotſwold hills riſing high above its level, give a continual ſupply of coolneſs and moiſture; while the over-ſevern diſtrict has no ſuch maſs of mountain riſing immediately behind it. The popular idea ſeems to be that the difference is owing to aſpect. The two, jointly,

jointly, may account for it. Diſtricts, every-where, vary as to climature: not altogether through latitude, aſpect, or elevation; but to ſome other cauſe or cauſes;---which are certainly intereſting ſubjects of inveſtigation. Much depends upon climature. A forwardneſs of ſeaſon is always deſirable. The value of land is materially influenced by the climature it lies in.

The SURFACE, an extended plane; ſwelling with gentle protuberances; and ſet with ſome hillocks of remarkable beauty. Church-Down (provincially "Choſen Hill") is, in beauty, next to Matſon's lovely hillock. But Wainlode hill, on the immediate bank of the Severn, commands the broadeſt, beſt view of the vale;---backed by its environing hills.

The common receptacle of the ſurface water of the diſtrict is the Severn: The collecting SHORES*, rivulets which croſs the vale.

The

* SHORE. This word has been cenſured by a critic whoſe remarks are entitled to attention: it is therefore proper to ſay that I do not uſe the word *ſhore*, as a corruption of *iſſue!* (Johnſon s idea) but as a word, (probably of ſome centuries ſtanding) *analogous* with *ſewer*; which, pronounced as it is written, is become a *provincialiſm*: while to write *ſewer*, and pronounce *ſhore* is an evident impropriety. The eſtabliſhed language has no inſtance analogous with ſuch a uſage.

The Severn being EMBANKED to confine its waters within due limits, during *minor* floods,---the rivulets are let into it by flood-gates, which give vent to them at dead water; and exclude the water of the river in times of floods *.

Near the banks of the Severn, an overflow of these rivulets may sometimes be irremediable; but the area of the district, in general, is placed, by natural situation, entirely out of the reach of surface water. Neverthelefs, much of it is effentially injured by water lodging upon it, during winter and wet feafons. The rivulets are fhamefully neglected; and the water ditches choaked for want of timely fcouring. A COMMISSION OF SHORES is evidently wanted in this diftrict, to free it from the evils of fuperfluous water; one of the moft ruinous

* SEVERN EMBANKMENT. This is not a *publick* work; nor is it general; the meadows being in many places ftill left open. The intention of it is merely to fecure the grafs from being filted, and the hay from being fwept away, by fummer floods. The banks being low; not more perhaps than two to three feet high; the winter's floods furmount them; or, if raifed higher, the water at that feafon is, I underftand, fometimes let into the meadows by fluices opened for that purpofe; fo that the meadows ftill receive a benefit from the floods.

ruinous enemies of hufbandry: yet, by proper management, it is, in general, the moft eafy to be overcome.

The SOIL of this diftrict is moftly a rich deep loam: fitted, by intrinfic quality, for the production of every vegetable fuited to its fpecific nature and the latitude it lies in. But by a redundancy of moifture it is chilled, weakened, and rendered much lefs productive than foils, which enjoy equal richnefs and equal depth, generally are. This is in part owing to a want of fufficient fhores, and furface-drains; and in part to the nature of the---

SUBSOIL, which accords with the theory above offered with refpect to climature: being in general fingularly cold and full of water; efpecially towards the center of the vale; where it appears, in many places, to be compofed of ftone and clay, alternately, in thin ftrata. And here, every ftone pit is a well of limpid water. There are parts of the diftrict, however, which enjoy a more genial foundation; efpecially round the towns of Glocefter, Tewkfbury and Evefham: fituations admirably well chofen. But no wonder; they were fixed upon, or raifed into eminence, by the clergy; who, it

is

is abundantly evident, were judges of ſoil and climature. The whole diſtrict under notice has been ſtrewed with monaſteries and other religious places.

The ROADS of the vale are ſhamefully kept. The Pariſh roads moſtly lie in their natural flat ſtate, with the ditches on either ſide of them full of water to the brim. The toll-roads are raiſed (generally much too high) but even on the ſides of theſe I have ſeen full ditches. It would, in principle, be equally wiſe to ſet a ſugar loaf in water by way of preſerving it, as to ſuffer water to ſtand on the ſides of roads whoſe foundations are of an earthy nature. For ſo long as they remain in immediate contact with water, they never can acquire the requiſite degree of firmneſs. The foundation is ever a quagmire; and the ſuperſtructure, if not made unneceſſarily ſtrong, is always liable to be preſſed into it. Hence the deep, ditch-like ruts which are commonly ſeen in roads of this deſcription. The road between Gloceſter, and Cheltenham (now become one of the moſt public roads in the iſland) is ſcarcely fit for the meaneſt of their Majeſties' ſubjects to travel on,---AND PAY FOR; much leſs ſuitable for their

their Majeſties themſelves, and their amiable family, to truſt their own perſons upon.

Materials are plentiful, and upon the ſpot. The ſtone of the ſubſoil is a blue-and-white limeſtone.---Lying, however, in thin ſtrata, ſeparated by thicker ſeams of clay, the raiſing of it is ſomewhat expenſive, and its duration is ſhort. But the ſhortneſs of the carriage ſtands againſt theſe diſadvantages. Below Gloceſter, the roads are made with "ſlag" copper droſs---and with the ſtone of St. Vincent's Rock near Briſtol. To forty or fifty miles of water-carriage, two or three of land carriage are not unfrequently added!

TOWNSHIPS. The only circumſtance noticeable, in this place, is the unfrequency of *alehouſes* in the townſhips of the vale: a circumſtance which reflects much honour on the magiſtracy of this county. Alehouſes are an intolerable nuiſance to huſbandry. They are the nurſeries of idleneſs, and every other vice. A virtuous nation could not, perhaps, be debauched ſooner, or with more certainty, than by planting alehouſes in it: yet we ſee them every where planted, as if for the purpoſe of rendering this nation more vicious than it already

ready is. If a reform of the lower clafs of people be really wifhed for, the firft ftep towards it would be, to fhut up the principal part of the petty alehoufes which are, at prefent, authorifed by Government to debauch them. Unfortunately, however, for fo defireable a reform, alehoufes, like lotteries, are opened " for the good of the nation"! The nation muft be in a tottering ftate, indeed, if it require gambling and drunkennefs, the two main pillars of vice, to fupport it *.

INCLOSURES. Many of the townfhips of this vale ftill lie in open common field--" common meadow "---and common paftures--provincially " Hams " which are ftinted for cows and other cattle. Perhaps half the vale is undivided property.

In the common arable fields, property is intermixed in a fingular manner. Not with a view

* From what will follow it may be faid that a want of alehoufes cannot prevent drunkennefs. In *this* country it certainly cannot. Neverthelefs this diftrict is a ftriking evidence that a fcarcity of alehoufes leffens the vices which feldom fail of affociating themfelves with *public* drunkennefs. There is a kind of *Pellewian* deportment obfervable among the lower clafs of people, in this diftrict, which I have not been able to difcover, in any other.

view to general conveniency or an equitable diſtribution of the lands to the ſeveral meſſuages of the townſhips they lie in, as in other places they appear to have been; but here the property of two men, perhaps neighbour's in the ſame hamlet, will be mixed land-for-land alternately; though the ſoil and the diſtance from the meſſuages be nearly the ſame.

A tradition which prevails in the diſtrict relates that this intermixture was made intentionally; to prevent the incloſure of the fields; and the crime is laid to the charge of the "Barons."

The circumſtances of intentional intermixture is probable; but the *Barons* were leſs likely to effect ſuch an expedient than the *Biſhops*; whoſe monaſteries were to be fed from the produce of the countries they ſeverally ſtood in. Roads in thoſe days were, in all probability, much worſe than they are now; and the buſineſs of diſtant carriage much more difficult than it is at preſent. *

C The

* Every monaſtery had its barn. Some of theſe barns, which appear to have been generally of immenſe ſize, are ſtill remaining. One of them, which I had the opportunity of obſerving, is in high preſervation; and ſtill in uſe as a barn. Over one of its porches is a room furniſhed with a fire

The monafteries being thus fituated, their exiftence depended on keeping a due portion of the lands in a ftate of ARATION. But the lands of this diftrict being better adapted, by the coolnefs of their fituation, to *grafs* than to *corn*, they were no fooner inclofed than converted to grafs-lands; and there appears to have been no other probable means of preventing their inclofure, than by cutting them into fhreds too fmall for that purpofe, and intermixing them in the manner in which they too evidently appear.

PRODUCE—principally *corn*. Befides the open fields, a confiderable fhare of the inclofures are arable. However, if we include the common meadows and ftinted paftures, nearly half the diftrict may be in *grafs*. The *woodland* is inconfiderable: not a hundred acres in the diftrict. I fpeak of the area of the vale. The Cotfwold cliffs, which overlook it, are partially hungw ith wood. Above Witcomb, on the fouthern limb of the circle, there is a charming tract of woodland. If more of this irregular cliff were planted; efpecially the fteeper

fire place and chimney; and opening into a gallery on the infide of the barn; probably for the conveniency of the barnward, in overlooking the workmen.

ſteeper bolder projections, which are now in a ſtate of waſte, the profit eventually might be conſiderable to the owner; while beechen mantles thrown over the preſent baldneſs of theſe projections could not fail of being grateful to the obſervers of rural beauty.

1.

ESTATES.

THIS DISTRICT includes no large eſtate.—Several Noblemen have off eſtates within it; but none of them is extenſive. The remainder belongs principally to reſident gentlemen; and to a pretty numerous yeomanry.

The TENURE is moſtly *fee-ſimple*; with ſome *copyhold*; and a conſiderable proportion of *Church leaſehold.* In the VALE OF EVESHAM, one third of the landed property is ſaid to be held by the laſt mentioned tenure:—moſtly by *leaſes for lives*;—two in poſſeſſion, and two in reverſion: ſome by *leaſes for a term*; as twenty one years, renewable every ſeven.

2.

THE GENERAL MANAGEMENT OF ESTATES.

THE DISTRICT more immediately under obſervation furniſhes little intereſting information on this head. There is no large eſtate in it to take the lead, and eſtabliſh a uniform ſyſtem of management.

The TENANCY is various: much of the vale remains *at will*. But *leaſes* are now become common, upon ſome of the off eſtates. The *term*—ſeven, fourteen or twenty one years.*

RENT.

* In the *vale of Eveſham*, in open-field townſhips, in which three crops and a fallow are the eſtabliſhed courſe of huſbandry—leaſes for four, eight, or twelve years; that is for one two or three courſes; are granted. This is a ſimple,

Rent. The old rent for grafsland 20s. for arable common-field 10s. an acre: landlord paying land tax; which, in moft cafes, runs very high in this diftrict. But eftates in general have been moderately raifed of late years. Grafsland now lets from 20s. to 30s. Common field land 10s. to 15s. Arable inclofures, and " every years' land " 10s. to 20s. an acre.

Covenants. Landlord *builds* and *repairs*. Tenant has the care of the *fences*: and is, in the cuftom of the country, allowed to lop and top *hedgerow timber*. *Gateftuff* is, I underftand, pretty generally allowed; and fometimes *plowboot*, *&c*. In the center of the vale, tenants are reftricted from felling *ftraw*; but, near the towns, they are not under this reftriction.

Receiving. The prevailing times of receiving are Michaelmas and Ladyday; landlords allowing their tenants fix months' credit.

ple, judicious principle of management, which might well be adopted in other arable diftricts, in which a regular courfe of hufbandry is eftablifhed: thus, in Norfolk, fix, twelve, or eighteen years would be a more eligible term of a leafe than feven, fourteen or twenty one;—the prefent term.

REMOVALS. Ladyday is the ufual time of changing tenants. Outgoing tenant fometimes holding part of the grafs grounds to old Mayday; and not uncommonly, I underftand, keeping poffeffion of the barns, &c. until the midfummer twelve-month following!:—Harvefting and thrafhing out all the corn fown upon the farm previous to his leaving it*.

FORMS OF LEASES. The following are the heads of a leafe in ufe on one of the firft off eftates in the diftrict.

LANDLORD AGREES to lett;—certain fpecified premifes; from Ladyday;—for a rent, and during a term, previoufly agreed upon.

ALSO to put the buildings into tenantable repair; and to keep them in repair during the term of the demife: (except as hereafter)

LANDLORD RESERVES all mines, quarries, coals, minerals, and metals; all timber, fruit and other trees, ftores, germins, and faplings; with

* How much preferable, in this refpect, is the *Norfolk* practice; in which the bufinefs of the farm goes on nearly in the fame manner, in the firft and the laft years of the leafe, as in any intermediate year; and in which the incoming tenant obtains full *poffeffion*, on the day of removal. (fee NORF: ECON:) For the practice of *Cleveland*; a diftrict very fimilar to this; fee YORK: ECON: vol I. p. 37.

with the lops, tops, and ſhredings thereof; together with all woods and underwoods, coppices, hedges, and hedgerows: (except as hereafter) with full liberty to ſearch for, cut down, &c. &c.

Also the right of hunting, fiſhing, and fowling; "and all other royalties whatſoever."

Also free liberty of viewing the premiſes, and doing repairs.

Also a liberty of planting timber or fruit trees, in hedgerows, or on "mounds;" that is, ditch banks.

Also to incloſe, or to exchange lands, without controul of the tenant; the difference in rental value to be eſtimated and fixed by arbitration.

Tenant agrees to take;—and to pay the ſtipulated rent, half yearly; within fourteen days after it be due;—under forfeiture of the leaſe.

Also to diſcharge all tithes, dues, levies, duties, rates, aſſeſſments, taxes, and payments, (the land tax only excepted) whether parliamentary or parochial, impoſed, or to be impoſed, on the premiſes.

Also to do ſuit and ſervice at the Lord's Court, holden for the manor in which the premiſes lie.

Also to do all neceſſary carriage for repairs.

Also to provide wheaten ſtraw, with rods, &c. for thatching.

Also to repair, and keep in good order and repair, and to deliver up in ſuch condition at the end of the term, the pump, and the windows, belonging to the premiſes.

Also the "court yards"—(including the ſtraw and dung yards)—with the cauſeways thereunto belonging.

Also to repair, keep and deliver up in good order and repair, the hedges, gates, pales, rails, ſtiles, mounds and fences; and to find iron work, ſpikes, and nails; (landlord providing and allowing rough timber;) for theſe purpoſes.

Also to ſcour and cleanſe the brook, ditches, watercourſes, drains, and pools; and the ſame to yield up at the end of the term in good and ſufficient order and repair.

Also to occupy, in himſelf or in his heirs, &c. all and every part of the premiſes: and not to aſſign, ſet-over, or lett, the whole, or

any

any parcel of them, (without the licence and conſent of the landlord) under forfeiture of the leaſe,

ALSO not to plow, dig, or break up any of the meadow or paſture ground, belonging to the premiſes;--under the penalty of ten pounds an acre, yearly, from the time of breaking up to the termination of the demiſe.

ALSO to grip, trench, hillock, and drain the graſs lands,

ALSO to fallow the arable land, every third or fourth year; according to the eſtabliſhed courſe of huſbandry of the townſhip it lies in.

ALSO to fold and pen on the premiſes, and not elſewhere, all ſuch ſheep as ſhall be kept thereon.

ALSO not to ſow hemp, flax, or rape ſeed on any part of the premiſes. NOR, otherwiſe, to croſs-crop: but to ſow the ſame corn and grain, from year to year, according to the beſt and moſt uſual courſe of huſbandry uſed in the reſpective townſhips*.

ALSO to rick and houſe upon the premiſes, all the corn, grain, and hay grown thereon.

AND

* The arable lands lie chiefly, or wholly in common fields.

And to ſpend and employ, on the ſame, all the ſtraw and fodder ariſing therefrom, in a huſbandlike manner. And to uſe on the premiſes, where moſt need ſhall require, and not elſewhere, all the muck, dung, ſoil, and compoſt riſing thereon. And not, in theſe or any other act or acts, negligently, wilfulfully, or willingly, impoveriſh or make barren, the lands under demiſe. Nor do or commit, or ſuffer to be done or committed, any waſte, ſpoil, or deſtruction whatſoever.

Also to plant ——— willows, (ſix for inſtance) yearly; on convenient parts of the premiſes; and to defend, and replace them, if neceſſary; under the penalty of 20s. a tree, yearly: landlord allowing rough timber for fencing*.

Also to preſerve and keep all ſuch trees as the landlord ſhall plant in the HEDGE-ROWS, *from ſpoil or damage by cattle* (after they have been once well fenced with timber by the landlord)

* This is a well conceived clauſe. In a vale diſtrict, deſtitute, in a manner, of woodlands, the WILLOW becomes a moſt uſeful tree: ſupplying the place of coppice wood, for rails, ſtakes, handles of tools, edders, withs, and, particularly in this diſtrict, for making a ſpecies of cattle crib, which will be hereafter deſcribed.

lord) AND in caſe any ſuch trees ſhall die, *by being hurt or ſpoiled by cattle*, to plant in their ſtead the like number, and the ſame ſorts and kinds; and theſe to preſerve and keep; under the penalty of 20s. a tree, yearly*.

ALSO,

* This likewiſe, *under due limitation*, is an admirable clauſe. Tempered with the Norfolk regulation in this caſe, it might be extended, *with propriety*, to PLANTATIONS, and be rendered highly beneficial to an eſtate, without being *alarming* to the tenants; though, in every caſe, it muſt in its nature be *hazardous*.

A clauſe of this kind,—ſeeing the difficulty of raiſing trees on old hedge-banks,—the uncertainty of ſeaſons, and the unſkilfulneſs of planters in general,—ought to be ſtrongly guarded, on the part of the tenant, in the ſpecification of the damage, for which the penalty ſhall be due; confining it ſolely to damage by cattle or other ſtock, or to other neglect, or wilful damage of the tenant.

The penalty, in this inſtance, appears to me imprudently high. An annual forfeiture of *one* ſhilling a tree would, during the uſual term of a leaſe, much more than repay the planting, and any increaſe of value, which could be expected in that time; and would be a ſufficient *check*, without being an *obſtacle*, to a good tenant.

My remarks on this clauſe are the fuller, as I have not met with it in the leaſes of any other diſtrict; and I am fully perſuaded, that, duly qualified, it would, if generally adopted, be highly advantageous to the landed intereſt. It avails little to plant; eſpecially in the hedgerows of off eſtates; unleſs the occupier be ſomeway intereſted in the ſucceſs of the plantation.

Also, *in the laſt year of the term*, to ſow ——— acres with clover ſeed (at the rate of 18lb. an acre) And ſuffer landlord, or in-coming tenant, to ſow the remainder of the barley land of that year, with that or other graſs ſeeds. And not, after the barley crop be cut, to plow in, or break up, or cut, mow, graze, or eat off the young clover, or any part thereof.

Also, *in the laſt year*, to weed, hoe, and cleanſe, and to ſuffer landlord, or incoming tenant, to weed, hoe, and cleanſe, the laſt, or "*going-off crop*."

Also to rick and houſe, and ſpend on the premiſes, and not elſewhere, all and every part of the "*going-off crop*;" and to leave in the courts and yards, all the manure made therefrom, for the uſe and benefit of the land-lord.

Also, *in the laſt year*, to deliver up, on the twenty firſt day of December, to the land-lord or incoming tenant,——— acres of the arable land;——as a fallow for the enſuing year.

Tenant to be allowed (over and above the rough timber for gates and fences) ſuf-ficient

ficient plow-boot, and fire-boot, neceſſary to be uſed in the management of the premiſes.

Also the laſt or "going-off crop" of corn and grain, ſown on the premiſes, in the laſt year of the term;—on ſuch land, and in ſuch kind and ſort, as come, in due courſe of huſbandry, to be ſown in that year*.

Also the uſe of the barns, and part of the out buildings and yards, for thraſhing out the grain, and ſpending the fodder of the laſt crop, during twelve months, after the expiration of the term.

FARM

* There is no condition made, in this diſtrict, nor, I believe, in this quarter of the kingdom, for the outgoing tenant to pay the rent and taxes (what in Yorkſhire is termed the onſtand) for his going-off crop: ſo that here (by long cuſtom) the outgoing tenant occupies, and receives the profits of, perhaps, three fourths of the arable land, after the term of general occupation ceaſes; while the incoming tenant is paying rent and taxes for it, without receiving any immediate advantage whatſoever from it. In *this* diſtrict, where wheat is ſown very late, Autumn, appears to me, evidently, the moſt eligible time of removal: And I have ſeen the copy of a leaſe, terminating at Michaelmas, in which the tenant agrees to plow the fallow field lands twice, and manure them in a huſbandlike manner, in the laſt year of the term; and to give up the reſt of the arable lands, and a part of the buildings, as ſoon as the laſt crops ſhall be off:—a mode of conducting the diſagreeable buſineſs under notice, greatly preferable, in my opinion, to that which is in more general practice.

3.

FARM BUILDINGS.

IMPROVEMENTS in rural architecture are not to be expected in the diftrict under furvey. Neverthelefs, the leading facts refpecting its FARM BUILDINGS require to be regiftered; and fome peculiarities, as well as fome few modern improvements, are entitled to notice.

MATERIALS. Timber appears to have been, formerly, the prevailing building-material of the diftrict. Farm buildings, in general, even to this day, are of frame-work; filled up with ftrong laths, interwoven in a peculiar manner, and covered with plaftering; or the ftudwork is covered with weather-boardery alone; efpecially outbuildings.

The prefent WALLING material is *brick*. Some few "*clay ftones*," dug out of the fubfoil, are ufed; and, under the hills, "*freeftone*"—a foft calcarious granate, which is common to the Cotfwold hills, is in ufe.

LIME

Lime is here a heavy article of building.—From 6d. to 8d. a bushel, of ten gallons level, at the kiln.

The stones, from which it is burnt, are brought by water carriage to the towns upon the Severn; either from Bristol, or from Westbury &c at the foot of the Forest of Dean; where the " claystone " of the subsoil is raised for this purpose. The kilns are built on the banks of the Severn; so that no land carriage of the stone is requisite. But the lime, notwithstanding the exorbitant price at the kiln is to be conveyed by land into the area of the district. The margin is supplied with the calcarious granate (which has been mentioned), from the Cotswold cliffs; and from Bredon hill; evidently a fragment of the Cotswolds.

These stones vary much in general appearance and contexture; and the limes produced from them are not less various in their qualities.

The " Bristol stone " has a somewhat flint-like appearance; is of a close, hard, and uniform contexture; and of a dark redish colour; sparkling with sparry particles; and flying under the hammer like glass: *no marine shell.*

One

One hundred grains of it afford forty five grains of air, and ninety ſeven grains of calcarious matter; leaving three grains of reſiduum;—a dark-coloured impalpable matter.* The lime produced from this ſtone burſts readily in water; and (like that produced from ſpars) is, when fallen, of a light floury nature: white as ſnow: covetted by the plaiſterer; but is conſidered by the maſon and bricklayer, as being of a *weak* quality.

The Weſtbury-ſtone—which is a ſufficient ſpecimen of the "clayſtones" found in the ſubſoil of moſt parts of the diſtrict—is in colour, contexture, and general appearance, very different from the rock of St. Vincent. It reſembles, in every reſpect, the marble-like limeſtone of the hills of Yorkſhire: generally blue at the core with a grey dirty-white cruſt: the baſe being of a ſmooth, even texture; *interſperſed with marine ſhells.* When it is freſh raiſed out of its watery bed in the area of the vale, it is a ſoft ſubſtance, of a ſomewhat ſoaplike appearance; but hardens (or falls to pieces)

* In ſolution it riſes to the ſurface as a black ſpume: on the filter it has the appearance of moiſtened ſoot: but adheres to the paper in drying.

pieces) on being expoſed to the atmoſphere. One hundred grains of this ſtone throw off forty grains of air; and afford ninety one grains of calcarious earth; leaving a reſiduum of nine grains;—an aſh-coloured ſilt. The lime burnt from it is characterized by *ſtrength*; and is high in eſteem for cement; being found ſtrong enough, in itſelf, to be uſed in water-work. It falls ſlowly; is of a ſomewhat brimſtone colour; and is diſtinguiſhed by the name of "brown lime." *

The

* Having obſerved the reluctance with which the lime of this ſpecimen (freſh from the kiln) imbibes water; while that of the Briſtol ſtone drinks it with ſingular avidity,—I was led to try, by a comparative experiment, whether their powers of imbibing air (that is of regaining their fixed air) were in like proportion. The reſult is intereſting.

One hundred grains of the firſt (in one knob) ſuſpended in a pair of ſcales, got full five grains in twenty four hours. In a drawer (which was ſometimes open, ſometimes ſhut) they got, in twenty four hours more, the ſame additional weight. In ſeven days more (wrapped in paper and lying in a drawer) they got twenty three grains: in all thirty three; or about three and a half grains a day: moſtly air, with, in all probability, ſome portion of water.

One hundred grains from the Weſtbury ſtone, placed in the drawer increaſed in twenty four hours not quite one grain! In twenty four hours more, in the ſcale, they barely made up a grain and a half! In ſeven days more they gained

 (in

The ſpecimen of *calcarious granate* which I have before me was taken from the middle of a " freeſtone quar ", within the " camp ", on Painſwick hill. It is common to the Cotſwold and the Lanſdown hills; and correſponds exactly with the ſoft limeſtone granate of Malton in Yorkſhire. It varies in ſpecific quality. The Bathſtone is ſofter and lighter than the ſpecimen under analyſis. One hundred grains of which diſcharge forty four grains of air; yielding ninety eight grains of ſoluble matter; and two grains of reſiduum; a ſnuff coloured impalpable matter. †

The method of *burning lime* in this country has nothing which entitles it to notice; except the

(in the drawer) exactly nine grains: in all ten and a half grains: not a grain and a quarter a day. Hence we may conceive how widely different may be the qualities of lime. Conſequently, how dangerous to draw general concluſions from an experiment, or even experiments, made with one particular ſpecies.

† It is proper to ſay that theſe experiments were made, and repeated, with great attention, and with exactly the ſame correſpondent reſults: nevertheleſs the *proportion of air to diſſoluble matter* varies in each ſpecimen. In the Briſtol ſtone the proportion is more than forty ſix, in the Cotſwold leſs than forty five,—in the Weſtbury leſs than forty four, to one hundred.

the practice of riddling and hand-picking the lime as it is drawn; to take out the ashes, cinders, and rubbish which may have been thrown into the kiln with the stones or coals. The labour is nor great; and the work is valuable. Lime as a building material; especially for the plasterer's use; cannot be too pure. The refuse pays the labourer, and the quantity of stone lime loses nothing by its absence.*

TIMBER. The old buildings of this district are full of fine oak; in which the lower lands of Glocestershire have heretofore, in all probability, been singularly abundant. But at present the vale is entirely stripped, and even the forest of Dean (some few parts of it excepted) is almost naked of good *oak timber*.

The vale, however, abounds at this time with *elm* of uncommon size and quality. This and foreign timber are the ordinary materials in

* The LIMEKILN of this district is noticeable, as being frequently furnished with a TOP, set upon the walls of the kiln, and contracted in a funnel-like form; the materials being carried in at a door in the side. In one instance, the kiln is built within a cone; in the manner of the brick kilns about London. The principal, if not the sole use of these tops, is to carry up the smoke and prevent its becoming a nuisance to the neighbourhood of the kilns.

uſe for farm buildings: oak being uſed only where durability is more particularly requiſite.

COVERING MATERIALS. An ordinary kind of *ſlate*, got out of the ſides of the hills, has formerly been the prevailing covering of the diſtrict. At preſent *knobbed plain tiles* are principally in uſe. The knob is an obvious improvement of the hole and pin; which are ſtill uſed about the metropolis.

Thatch is ſtill in uſe for cottages and farm-buildings. A ſpecies of thatch *new* to the reſt of the kingdom is here not unfrequently made uſe of; eſpecially near the towns, where wheat ſtraw is permitted to be ſold. In theſe ſituations, not only ricks; but *roofs*; are thatched with STUBBLE: a material which is found to laſt much longer than ſtraw; unleſs this be " helmed "; that is, have the heads cut off before thraſhing, in the Somerſetſhire manner: a practice which is not common in this country. That ſtubble ſhould be found to endure is reaſonably imagined. It has the advantage of helm (in not being bruiſed by the flail) and conſiſts of the ſtouteſt part of the ſtems. In many diſtricts it would be difficult to be uſed on account of its ſhortneſs; but in this

this country, where it is cut eighteen inches or perhaps two feet high, and (in the ſituations where it is more frequently uſed) has generally a ſufficient quantity of long wirey graſs among it to hold it together; there is no great difficulty in thatching with it: except in the raking; which requires a tender hand. It is firſt driven up a little with the teeth of the rake; beaten; and then raked gently downward.

FLOORING MATERIALS. Upper floors have heretofore been laid with *oak*; which is ſtill common in the floors and ſtair-caſes of all old houſes. *Elm* has, perhaps, been more recently uſed, and is ſtill in uſe, for the ſame purpoſes. Ground floors are not unfrequently of common *bricks* (a vile material for floors) or of "foreſt ſtone"—an excellent freeſtone grit, raiſed in the foreſt of Dean.

FARMERIES. The farm-buildings and yards, of the diſtrict under ſurvey, have not much to recommend them to particular notice. The arrangement has ſeldom any obvious deſign. There are however ſome few exceptions.

The BARNS of the vale are, in ſize below par: except the monaſtery barns already mentioned. There are few modern barns: the beſt, which has fallen under my obfervation, meafures thirty fix by eighteen feet on the infide ;—and the plate twelve feet high. The foundation brick. The fhell elm weather-boarding. The covering knobbed plain-tiles, twelve inches by feven ; laid in coarfe mortar ; with four and a half inch gage. The roof, behind, continued down to a plate fix feet high, fupported by pofts of elm fet on ftone ; forming an open fhed for cattle to reft under.

The BARN FLOOR of the diftrict is moftly of *plank* ; or of *foreft-ftone* ; which makes an admirable floor for beans ; and nor a bad one for barley: even wheat, with due care in keeping the ears bedded among ftraw, to prevent the flail from breaking the grain, may be thrafhed on a ftone floor with propriety. Clay floors are here in low efteem. The price of a ftone floor, compleat, is about 5d. a foot.

I fee nothing elfe in the farm-buildings of this vale which is entitled to defcription ; except BULLOCK STALLS, which are here built in what will no doubt be deemed a fuperb ftyle, by thofe who have been accuftomed to lefs coftly buildings for the fame purpofe: and CALF STAGES ; an admirable conveniency ; which

which is peculiar, I believe, to the diſtrict; but which ought to be univerſally known; as it may, in any breeding country, be adopted with ſingular propriety.

But deſcriptions of theſe conveniences will fall better under the articles to which they reſpectively belong; namely REARING CATTLE and FATTING CATTLE: ſubjects which will be duly noticed in their places.

The CIDERMILL HOUSE, an erection almoſt as neceſſary as a barn, upon a Glocesterſhire farm, will likewiſe be deſcribed under its proper head.

STACK STAGES are here very common. Moſtly upon ſtone pillars and caps. The price 18d. to 2s. a pair. A ſmall, but ſnug frame, is here made with five pillars. Four ſet quadrangularly, and one in the center. By making the outſide of the frame ſomewhat compaſſing, round ſtacks are conveniently enough ſet on theſe ſquare ſtages.

YARD FENCES are almoſt invariably *broad rails*; the Norfolk battons. Under theſe fences a line of STRAW-MANGERS are uſually formed: and, in the area of the yards, CRIBS of various conſtructions are in uſe.

4.

FIELD-FENCES.

OLD LIVEHEDGES are the ordinary fences of the diſtrict. The preſent incloſures, if we may judge from the age of their hedges, are probably ſome centuries old.

In the MANAGEMENT of live fences, whether young or old, I have met with nothing, here, that is entitled to particular notice.

It is, however, obſervable, in this place, that one of the fineſt hedges I have ſeen in the diſtrict, grows on a cold unproductive ſwell: the land not worth, though incloſed, 10s. an an acre: yet, on land worth twice that rent, I have ſeldom ſeen a hedge grow ſo luxuriantly. A ſufficient evidence, that, *in the valuing of land*, HEDGES cannot be depended upon, as criterions to judge from. The hedge may feed in a fertilizing ſubſoil, which corn, or the better graſſes, may not be able to reach.

The DITCHES, in every part of the vale, are ſhamefully neglected! A vale diſtrict, without deep clean ditches, reflects diſgrace on on the owners, as well as on the occupiers, of its lands. In a diſtrict, that, by natural ſituation, is too cold and moiſt, every poſſible means ought to be uſed to free it from ſurface water: which, if it ſtand only an hour upon the ſoil; or in immediate contact with it; adds, more or leſs, to its natural coldneſs.

The ordinary TEMPORARY FENCE is bar hurdles.

GATES are here made low; with a ſtrong top-bar, in the Kentiſh manner; but want the long upper eye or thimble of the Surrey-Gate*.

STILES are ſingularly abundant. They appear frequently to be placed merely as preſervatives of the hedges; and this may, in many caſes, be good policy. They are frequently made *to open:* the top rail having an iron bolt driven through it, at one end; the other end falling into a notch in the oppoſite poſt, making an opening wide enough to paſs a carriage through occaſionally.

HEDGEROW

* HANGING GATES. In this diſtrict, it is the invariable practice to drive the hooks into the *corner* of the poſts, and the thimbles into the *corner* of the hartree; which, in this caſe, ſhuts within the poſt.

5.

HEDGEROW TIMBER.

THE HEDGE TREES of the vale are moſtly ELM and WILLOW. Few of OAK or ASH.

The MAPLE, which grows unuſually large, here, is conſidered as a timber tree, and is put to many uſes for which, in other diſtricts, it is not deemed ſuitable. But the nature of the ſoil, or the variety which is here cultivated, may render its texture leſs brittle than it generally is, in other diſtricts. Hurdles, gates, and even ciderpreſs ſkrews are made of it.

The ELM (chiefly the fine-leaved elm) grows with uncommon luxuriance, and to an unuſual ſize, in the vale ſoil. Its progreſs is quickeſt on the lighter warmer lands; but here the trees ſooneſt decay, and the timber is of the leaſt value. In ſtiffer, more clayey ſituation, its growth is leſs rapid; but its timber is of a much better quality: the colour of iron; and, in ſome inſtances, almoſt as hard. —The

—The Briſtol ſhip-builders have a ſupply of keel-pieces from this quarter; and I know no country, which is ſo likely to furniſh good ones.

The vales of Gloceſterſhire may boaſt of three of the moſt remarkable trees in the iſland, PIFFE'S ELM, the BODDINGTON OAK, and the TORTWORTH CHESNUT;—but having deſcribed them fully in another work, I forbear to particularize them here*.

Hedgerow timber is univerſally *lopped*; few, however, are *beaded* low in the pollard manner; except WILLOWS; which, as has been ſaid, are here, conſidered in a degree neceſſary to every farm.

* See PLANTING and ORNAMENTAL GARDENING; articles FAGUS: QUERCUS: ULMUS.

6.

WOODLANDS.

COPPICES are the only natural woodlands of the area of the vale. Of theſe there are two or three: one of them, in the center of the vale, is of conſiderable extent.

Part of this coppice is a COMMON WOOD;—*appropriated* to the meſſuages of the townſhip it belongs to, but not *divided:* ſomewhat analogous with common fields and common meadows. A ſpecies of property I have not met with elſewhere.

It is obſervable that, in a part of this coppice, ſome ſtandard oaks are left as timber trees; which, contrary to common practice, are lopped to the top (as hedgerow trees) every time the coppice wood is cut. This certainly leſſens their hurtfulneſs to the underwood; but the timber becomes, no doubt, of a very inferior quality. Their crop of fuel, however, every fifteen or twenty years, muſt be conſiderable.

conſiderable. The queſtion is whether, on the whole, they are, or are not, more profitable than coppice wood alone: and it appears to me, on reflection, to be a diſputable queſtion. It probably hinges on whether the trees feed below or among the roots of the coppice-wood.

This patch of woodland is further entitled to notice.—The *ſoil* is an unproductive clay, mixt with and bottomed by a thin ſeam of calcarious gravel; lying on a cold clayey ſubſoil; not worth, as arable land, more than 8s. an acre: not eſtimated in this country at more than 5s. an acre.

The *ſpecies* of wood is principally *oak*, *aſh*, and *maple*, with ſome *ſallow*, *white-thorn*, and *hazle*. The *uſes* to which it is applyed are principally rails, hurdle-ſtuff,—hedging materials, and fuel. The *age of felling* twenty years. And its eſtimated *value* at that age, twelve to fifteen pounds an acre! Its growth is uncommonly luxuriant: the ſtools are thick upon the ground; and, being cut high, afford numerous ſhoots. In the latter ſtages of its growth, it is the moſt impenetrable thicket I have ſeen; while the crops of corn and graſs, which

which border upon it, are remarkably weak and unproductive.

This shows, in a striking manner, the judgment requisite in laying out estates: giving such lands to husbandry, as are adapted to its productions; and converting to woodland, such as are naturally prone to wood.

7.

PLANTING.

THE PLANTATIONS of the vale consist wholly of fruit-trees. Forest-trees may be said to be here in total neglect; excepting some few ashen coppices for cider-cask hoops; a species of plantation common on the Herefordshire side of the county.

If, however, we may judge from the coppice which has been spoken of above; and the hedge noticed aforegoing; it is highly probable,

bable, that many of the cold ſwells, which occur in different parts of the vale, might be planted with great profit.

The timber-oak is, at preſent, almoſt entirely baniſhed from *this* ſide of the Severn; and although the oppoſite banks are, yet, ſufficiently wooded; the preſent woods will, in all probability, be fallen, long before ſuch as may be now raiſed from the acorn, will be ready for the axe.

FARMS.

8.

FARMS.

THE PREVAILING CHARACTERISTIC of farms, in this diſtrict, is a mixture of graſs and arable land; in various proportions. Near the towns of Gloceſter and Tewkeſbury, there are ſome few large farms, "all green:"—that is, conſiſting entirely of graſs-land. But this, alone, makes an inconvenient farm; eſpecially in a dairy country, where litter and winter fodder, for dry cows and rearing cattle, are requiſite.

The exact proportion of arable to graſs, however, does not ſeem to be fixed. Too much graſs gives a ſcarcity of ſtraw: too much arable interferes with the dairy; or, perhaps, more accurately ſpeaking, the dairy interferes with much arable land. Even in harveſt, let the weather be what it may, the buſineſs of milking and the dairy muſt be attended to.

Hence,

Hence, perhaps, we may conclude, that corn and the dairy ought not to *rival* each other: one of them ought to be *ſubordinate*; ought to be rendered ſubſervient to the MAIN OBJECT of management. *

In regard to SIZE, the vale farms are of the middle caſt. From one to three hundred acres is, I believe, the moſt prevalent ſize. There are ſome made-up farms of much higher magnitude; but no entire farm, in the area of the vale, lets, I underſtand, for more than four hundred pounds a year: not many, I believe, higher than two hundred a year. †

PLAN. Some of theſe larger farms; moſt of them "manor" or "court" farms; or ſimply "the farm" with the name of the townſhip affixed to it; (undoubtedly the ancient

* Neverthelefs, a profeſſional man, whoſe knowledge of the practice of the diſtrict entitles him to be heard with deference, gives the following as the beſt proportion of a farm, in the VALE OF EVESHAM: fifty two acres of arable, (ſubjected to three crops and a fallow) with ſixty acres of paſture ground, and thirty acres of meadow.

† The ſame ſuperior manager is of opinion, that a double farm of the deſcription given in the laſt note is the beſt ſize; and that larger farms are, in the vale, dangerous both to landlord and tenant.

cient demeſne lands of the townſhips they reſpectively lie in); are very entire; and lie well round the homeſteads. But farm houſes, in general, ſtand in villages; the lands belonging to them being ſtill ſcattered about in the extraordinary manner which has been deſcribed. How wrong in their owners *now* to continue them in that unprofitable ſtate. The loſs falls wholly on themſelves. They let at a rent proportioned to their preſent diſadvantages.

9.

FARMERS.

HUSBANDMEN are much the ſame in all diſtricts: plain, frugal, pains-taking, cloſe, and unintelligible. The lower and middle claſs of farmers, of the diſtrict under obſervation, moſtly anſwer, in a remarkable manner, to this deſcription:—while ſome few of the ſuperior claſs are as ſtrongly marked by liberality and communicativeneſs:—characters which begin to adorn ſuperior farmers in every diſtrict;

diſtrict; and which muſt, eventually, do more toward the perfection of the art, than all the applauded ſchemes which theory can boaſt. Theoriſts may draw plans, and ſuggeſt hints; and in ſo doing may do good ſervice. But profeſſional men, only, can execute, correct, mature, and introduce them into general practice. Should profeſſional men become ſcientific as well as liberal, what may not be expected? And who, viewing the riſing generation, many of them opulent, well educated, and duly initiated in the profeſſion they are deſigned for, can apprehend that none of them will become ſtudious of the art which alone can render them uſeful and reſpectable in ſociety?

10.

WORKMEN.

FARM LABOURERS are ſufficiently numerous.--they are noticeable as being ſimple, inoffenſive, unintelligent, and apparently ſlow. How different from the farm labourers of Norfolk!

Their wages are very low, *in money*; being only 1s. a-day. But, *in drink*, ſhamefully exorbitant. Six quarts a day the common allowance: frequently two gallons: ſometimes nine or ten quarts; or an unlimited quantity.

In a cider year the *extravagance* of this abſurd cuſtom (which prevails throughout the cider country) is not perceived. But now (1788) after a ſucceſſion of bad fruit years, it is no wonder the farmers complain of being beggared by malt and hops! They are not, however, entitled to pity. The fault—the crime—is their own. If a few leading men, in each townſhip, would agree to reduce the quantity of labourers' drink within due bounds, it would at once be effected.

But the origin of the evil, I fear, reſts with themſelves. In a fruit year, cider is of little value. It is no uncommon circumſtance to ſend out a general invitation, into the highways and hedges; in order to empty the caſks, which were filled laſt year, that they may be refilled this. A habit of drinking is not eaſily corrected. Nor is an art learnt in youth readily forgot. Men and maſters are equally adepts in the art of drinking. The tales which are told

told of them are incredible. Some two or three I recollect. But, although I have no reason to doubt the authorities I had them from, I wish not to believe them: I hope they are not true.

Drinking a gallon-bottle-full at a draught is said to be no uncommon feat. A mere boyish trick, which will not bear to be bragged of. But to drain a two-gallon bottle without taking it from the lips, as a labourer of the vale is said to have done, by way of being even with master, who had paid him short in *money*—is spoken of as an exploit, which carried the art of draining a wooden bottle to its full pitch. Two gallons of cider, however, are not a stomach-full. Another man of the vale undertook, for a trifling wager, to drink twenty pints, one immediately after another. He got down nineteen (as the story is gravely told) but these filling the cask to the bung, the twentieth could not of course get admittance: so that a Severn-man's stomach holds exactly two gallons three pints.

But the quantity drank, in this extempore way, by the men, is trifling, compared with that which their masters will swallow at a sitting.

ting. Four well ſeaſoned yeomen, (ſome of them well known in *this* vale) having raiſed their courage with the juice of the apple, reſolved to have a freſh hogſhead tapped; and, ſetting foot to foot, emptied it at one ſitting.

11.

BEASTS OF LABOUR.

HORSES are at preſent, the only beaſts of draught, in the vale.

Formerly ſome OXEN were worked in it, double, in yoke; but they were found to poach the land, and were on that account, given up. But now, when oxen are worked, on almoſt every ſide of it, ſingle, as horſes, it is ſomewhat extraordinary they ſhould not be admitted into the vale: where their keep would be ſo eaſy: where graſs and hay may be had at will.

The objection ſtill held out againſt them is, that, even ſingle, they tread the vale lands too much. But in this I ſuſpect there is a ſpice of obſtinacy in the old way: a want of a due

due portion of the ſpirit of improvement: a kind of indolence: It might not, perhaps, be too ſevere to ſay of the vale farmers, that they would rather be eaten up by their horſes, than ſtep out of the beaten tract to avoid them.

In harrowing wide ridges, in a wet ſeaſon, oxen may be leſs eligible than horſes. But ſhoeing them with whole ſhoes, as horſes, might remedy the comparative evil. If not—let thoſe who are advocates for oxen calculate the comparative difference in *wear* and keep; and thoſe who are their enemies, eſtimate the comparative miſchiefs of treading; and thus decide upon their value as beaſts of labour in the vale. *

If after a *fair trial* oxen be ineligible;—let the preſent *waſte of horſes* be leſſened. Uſing five horſes to a plow, in ſtirring a looſe loamy fallow, not more perhaps than four or five inches deep, is a crime againſt the community, that ought to be puniſhable. In the firſt plowing of a fallow; as well as in plowing for beans or wheat; ſix, and not unfrequently ſeven horſes, at-length, are uſed to *one* plow! Yet theſe five

E 4 ſix

* I am told, that in the VALE OF EVESHAM, they are gradually coming into uſe.

ſix or ſeven horſes; with one or two men, and one or two boys; ſeldom plow three quarters of an acre a day; two thirds of an acre is the day's work of the country! But the plow, in uſe, is a diſgrace to preſent huſbandry: thirteen to fourteen feet long, and heavy in proportion.

I am well aware that ſtrong land, plowed deep, as it is in this diſtrict, requires a ſtrong team; and that a long plow is *convenient to the plowman*; eſpecially in laying up high ſteep ridges. But ſimilar ridges are laid up, in the midland counties, with a ſhort plow and three horſes. And I know, from experience or adequate obſervation, in various parts of the iſland, that, allowing for the nature of the ſoil, and the aukwardneſs of the ridges, there is an evident and great waſte of plow horſes in the diſtrict under notice. Six horſes, worth perhaps from twenty to thirty pounds each, are not expected to work more than fifty or ſixty acres of arable land (with a greater or leſs proportion of graſs land annexed to it.) If theſe fifty or ſixty acres be common field land, the intereſt of the firſt coſt, the annual *wear*, and the

the hazard—incident to ſuch ſix horſes, amount nearly to the rental value of the land: and their keep, if they be properly kept up, is worth twice or three times its rental value.

12.

IMPLEMENTS.

THE GLOCESTERSHIRE WAGGON is, beyond all argument, the beſt farm-waggon I have ſeen in the kingdom.—I know not a diſtrict which might not profit by its introduction. Its moſt ſtriking peculiarity is that of having a crooked ſide-rail, bending archwiſe over the hind wheel. This lowers the general bed of the waggon, without leſſening the diameter of the wheels. The body is wide, in proportion to its ſhallowneſs; and the wheels run ſix inches wider than thoſe of the Yorkſhire waggon, whoſe ſide-rail is ſix inches higher. Its advantages, therefore, in carrying a top-load are obvious. (ſee YORKS: ECON: on this ſubject, vol I. p. 269) And, for

for a body-load, it is much the ftiffeft beft waggon I have feen. The price 20 to 25l. according to the fize, and the ftrength of the tire. The weight, 15 Cwt. to a ton.

This waggon is common to Glocefterfhire and to North-Wiltfhire. How much farther it extends weftward, I know not. It is a ftranger in the fouthern, the eaftern, the northern and the midland counties.

Where, and by whom it was firft invented, I have not learned. It is fometimes called the Cotfwold waggon. It is, by way of preeminence, well entitled to the name of the Farmers' waggon: for I have not feen another, which, compared with this, is fit for a farmer's ufe.

SEASONS.

13.

SEASONS.

THE PROGRESS OF SPRING, in 1788, in the vale of Glocester.

Sallow in full blow—4 April.
Sloe-thorn in blow—11 April.
Hawthorn foliated—16 April.
Cuckoo firft heard—20 April.
Elm foliated—21 April.
Pear tree in full blow—27 April.
Swifts—28 April!*
Houfe-marten—30 April.
Swallows—1 May.
Thermometer—76.° in the fhade—1 May!
Apple tree in full blow—3 May.
Oak foliated—4 May.
Afh foliated—5 May.
Thunder—6 May.
Hawthorn began to break 10th; in full blow—17 May.

The

* This is a remarkable circumftance. On the 29th of April SWIFTS were in number, flying high in the atmofphere, before a fingle SWALLOW had made its appearance. The

The only circumſtance noticeable, with reſpect to the WEATHER of this year, is that of its *extreme dryneſs*. From the beginning of July to the cloſe of the year, there has been a continuation of dry weather; excepting two or three days' rain in September.

Springs have ſeldom been known ſo low, as they are at preſent (Jan. 1789.) Nature's ſtore rooms appear to be exhauſted. Even in this watery vale, ſurface ſprings, in general, and moſt wells, have been dry ſome months; water having been fetched, and cattle driven, a conſiderable diſtance. The reſervoirs on the ſkirts of Matſon hill, for ſupplying the city of Gloceſter with water, have been empty many weeks: a circumſtance unknown before.

This want of rain, here, is the more remarkable, as throughout a great part of Wales, not fifty miles diſtant, ſummer and autumn were rainy, almoſt without interruption!

In the middle of October, while the lands of this country were ſo dry, that they could not

The weather unuſually warm. A ſtrong evidence, that the ſwift does *not* migrate. It ſeldom miſtakes the ſeaſon, like the ſwallow. We rarely ſee a ſwift, before the ſpring be confirmed.

not, with any propriety, be worked for wheat; and while, even in Herefordshire, farmers were breaking the clots with beetles; the farmers in Wales, not twenty miles distant, had not been able to put a plow into the ground for near a month, owing to the excessive wetness of the season! While in Yorkshire, having been missed by the rain of September, which gave a loose to the grass in this district, the stinted pastures had been so bare, the cattle had been foddered in them!

These circumstances, so remarkable, and so nearly connected with our subject, I could not pass over unnoticed. *Showers*, or *a few days' rain*, not unfrequently fall in a partial manner:—but I never before knew a *long-continued rainy season*, which was not common to the kingdom.

GENERAL

14.

GENERAL MANAGEMENT OF FARMS.

VIEWING the vale as one farm, its objects of management are the four grand objects of hufbandry:

Corn;
Breeding;
The Dairy;
Fatting.

There are fome few individual farms, applied, principally, *to grazing:* others chiefly to the *dairy:* and there may be fome few fmall *arable* farms. But upon the larger farms, in general, the four objects are held in view.

The ARABLE CROPS are principally WHEAT, BARLEY, BEANS; with fome *peas*, and a *few oats!* Alfo, of late years, fome *clover*, *vetches*, and fome few *turneps* have been cultivated*. It

* TURNEPS. In the center of the vale, there are few or none grown. The reafon given is, they cannot be got off the land: and, while the country remains without roads and

It may, however, be ſaid, with little latitude, that NATURAL HERBAGE is, in this diſtrict, the only SUBORDINATE CROP.

From what has gone before, it may, perhaps, be conceived, that the ARABLE MANAGEMENT of this diſtrict, cannot be entitled to particular notice. This, however, would be deciding too raſhly. The rural management of a country reſembles the moral character. I have not found one that is perfect: nor one which does not comprize ſome portion of good. The arable management, of the country under ſurvey, appears to the obſerver in light and ſhade; and exhibits ſome traits, which the reader, I think, will not be diſpleaſed with. Beſides, in it, we have a ſpecimen of the practice of a claſs of country, which includes a conſiderable ſhare of the beſt lands of this quarter

and ſurface drains, this muſt neceſſarily be the caſe; eſpecially where the ſoil is ſtrong, tenacious, and cold; a ſoil altogether unfit for turneps. There are, however, lands in the vale, well adapted to this crop; and its abſence implies, either a want of the ſpirit of improvement, or no need of *cultivated herbage*. In a vale country, abounding with graſs-lands, turneps are of leſs value, than they are in a hilly country, deſtitute of *natural herbage*. If *arable herbage* were wanted in the vale, CABBAGES would probably be found more eligible than turneps.

ter of the iſland: namely ARABLE VALE. A ſketch of it appears, to me, eſſentially neceſſary, in a REGISTER OF THE PRESENT STATE OF ENGLISH AGRICULTURE. The reader may reſt aſſured, that, for my own eaſe and gratification, as well as his, I will not dwell longer on the ſubject, than the general deſign of the work I am executing requires.

15.

COURSE OF HUSBANDRY.

THE ANCIENT COURSE of the common fields was the ſame, here, as in moſt other diſtricts: namely,

Fallow,

Wheat, &c.

Beans, &c.—And to this ancient courſe, ſeveral of the townſhips of the vale ſtill adhere.

But ſome townſhips in *this* vale, and many, I believe, in the *vale of Eveſham*, have, of late years, changed the ancient ſyſtem of management; for one, which, ſingular as it may appear

appear to thoſe, who have been accuſtomed to fallow for wheat, is founded on good principles; and might well be copied by other ſtiff-ſoiled, open-field townſhips: namely,

Fallow;
Barley;
Beans, or clover;
Wheat.

The reaſons given for this change (this ſtriking and ſingular effort, this promiſing dawn of improvement) are,—the bean crop, in the old courſe, came round too quick; the wheat did not do ſo well, after fallow, as after beans;—nor the beans ſo well, after wheat, as after barley.

Some farmers throw in CLOVER, inſtead of beans, between the barley and the wheat crops.

In the neighbourhood of Glocester, are ſome extenſive common fields, under an extraordinary courſe of management. They have been cropped, year after year, during a century, or perhaps centuries; without one intervening whole year's fallow. Hence they are called "EVERY YEAR'S LAND*."

On

* Cheltenham, Deerhurſt, and ſome few other townſhips, have likewiſe their "EVERY YEAR'S LANDS."

On theſe lands no REGULAR SUCCESSION of crops is obſerved; except that a "brown and a white crop"—pulſe and corn—are cultivated in alternacy.

The incloſed arable lands are under a ſimilar COURSE OF MANAGEMENT.

16.

SOILS AND TILLAGE.

THE SPECIES OF SOILS have been mentioned as various. Near the towns of Glocester and Tewkeſbury, a DEEP RICH LOAM prevails. Round Cheltenham, a DEEP SAND. The riſing grounds of Deerhurſt are covered with a RED LOAM; a remarkable ſpecies of ſoil; common to the hillocks of the over-Severn diſtrict, and to the inferior hills of Herefordſhire. It is here called RED LAND;" and reſembles much the "RED HILLS" of Nottinghamſhire

The area of the vale is a DEEP LOAM; of various degrees of richneſs and contexture. In the center of it, a remarkable ſpecimen of vale land appears: a patch of CALCARIOUS GRAVEL: partaking of the nature of the Cotſwold ſoil!

The particulars noticeable in the SOIL PROCESS of this diſtrict, relate ſolely to TILLAGE: namely,

1. Breaking up graſs land.
2. Fallowing.
3. Laying up ridges.

I. BREAKING UP GRASS LAND. This is not a common operation; yet it ſometimes takes place: At preſent, there are many inſtances, in which it is much wanted. Old paſture lands, over-run with ant-hills, and the coarſer graſſes, are not eaſily reclaimed, without the powerful aſſiſtance of the plow.

The method of performing the operation, in this diſtrict, is by no means intended to be held out as a pattern. It has, however, ſufficient pretenſions to a place in this regiſter.

It varies in the firſt ſtages: ſometimes the ant-hills are cut off, carried into heaps, and mixt with ſtraw, &c. as manure for corn land. Sometimes they are dried and burnt. But,

 in

in the prevailing practice of the country, the ſward and ant-hills are plowed up together, in the ſpring. In ſummer, the land has *one* croſs plowing. In autumn the ſurface is reduced and levelled; with the harrow; ſown with wheat; and the ſeed buried with the plow, among the graſs-roots and ant-hills.

The enſuing autumn,—the crop being reaped, and the ſtubble mown and raked off,—the ſoil is turned over, and ſown again, (and perhaps a third time), with wheat on one plowing! There has, I am told, been inſtances,—there has (I think I am well informed) been at leaſt one inſtance, of wheat being thus repeatedly ſown (upon a piece of extraordinaryly good land) ſix years, ſucceſſively; the laſt crop being ſaid to be nearly as good as the firſt!!! This, while it diſcovers the indiſcretion of the farmer, evinces the natural ſtrength of the vale lands, and ſhows, in a ſtriking light, the value of old-paſtured turf as a matrice for wheat.

II. QUANTITY OF TILLAGE. In the common fields which are under the improved plan of cultivation,—the number of plowings, in the four years round, is ſix. Three in the fallow

low year: one for barley: one for beans: and, generally, one for wheat.

The fallow is broken up after barley feed time; flitting the ridges *down*, by a deep plowing. In the firft ftirring, they are gathered *up*. On this fecond plowing, the manure is fpread; and plowed under with a fhallow furrow; which is, likewiife, turned *upward*; to lay the ridges dry during winter. In the fpring, they are flit *down*, for barley; and, next autumn, gathered *up*, for beans; and the enfuing autumn, again plowed *upward*, for wheat. Six plowings in four yearts, for three crops and a fallow; four of them being *upward*, two *downward*, of the ridges. Sometimes the bean ftubble is pared down very thin, previous to the feed-plowing for wheat. But fometimes the fallow has only two plowings.

With this fmall quantity of tillage, it is no wonder that even the barley ftubbles fhould be foul; or that the bean crop, notwithftanding the extraordinary care which is taken of it, fhould, in fome feafons, be half fmothered in weeds; or that the wheat ftubbles, notwithftanding the fingular attention which is paid to the crop while growing, fhould, not unfrequently, be knee-deep in couch and thiſtles.

Two or three plowings of ſuch ſtubbles are not entitled to the name of a *fallow*: they are juſt ſufficient to break the roots of couch graſs and thiſtles into ſets, as it were to propagate and increaſe, rather than to leſſen, their number. While ſeed-weeds, of every genus, are ſuffered to mature, and ſhed their ſeeds, between the plowings. A more ingenious way of propagating weeds would be difficult to conceive.

Fortunately, however, for the character of the vale, as an arable country, this diſgraceful management, though prevalent, is not univerſal. I have ſeen land, in various parts of it, in a high ſtate of tillage, and beautifully clean. But, even for this, I cannot allow an occupier any great ſhare of *merit*; it is little more than his *duty* as a huſbandman. In keeping land clean and in tilth, and taking a crop every year, ſkill, as well as induſtry, is required, and merit is of courſe due. But to keep it in a huſbandly ſtate, with a whole ſummer's fallow, every third or fourth year, wants common induſtry only: and a man, who with this

this opportunity, fuffers his crops to be impaired, through a want of fufficient tillage, ought not to be entrufted with the occupation of arable land.

If, however, we fee caufe of cenfure, in a redundancy of weeds, and want of tillage, in the fields, which are fallowed every third or fourth year,—what fhall we expect to find in the fields, which are never fallowed? Where *barley* is looked up to as the *cleanfing crop*! I wifh not to exaggerate; and to defcribe their ftate of foulnefs, with accuracy, would be difficult, or impoffible. I will, therefore, only fay, that I have found beans hid among muftard feed, growing wild as a weed, but occupying the ground as a crop;—peas, languifhing under a canopy of the cornmarigold and the poppies;—barley, with fcarcely a ftem free from the fetters of the convolvulus;—and wheat, pining away, plant after plant, in thickets of couch and thiftles.

In the language of cenfure I have no gratification. But, could I pafs over, unnoticed,—or, having feen, could be filent on—management fo highly blameable,—I fhould be altogether unfit for the tafk I have undertaken.

It is more than probable that one third of the crops, collectively, of ſome of the beſt-ſoiled fields in the diſtrict, is every year *loſt*, through a WANT OF SUFFICIENT TILLAGE.

Theſe circumſtances are mentioned with more readineſs, and with greater freedom; as every diſtrict of the kingdom lies more or leſs open, to ſimilar cenſure; and I make uſe of this opportuity of mentioning them; becauſe no other diſtrict, I have examined, affords evidences ſo ſtriking, as theſe which are here produceable.

It might not be far wide of the truth to ſay, that one fourth of the produce of the arable lands of the kingdom is *loſt* through a WANT OF TILLAGE: yet I find men in every country *afraid* to make a whole year's fallow, leſt they ſhould leſſen their produce! But let thoſe who are adverſe to fallowing, come here and be convinced of the magnitude of their error.

If land be in a ſtate of foulneſs, with root-weeds,—as half of the old arable lands of the kingdom may be ſaid to be,—a year's fallow is the *ſhorteſt*,—the moſt effectual,—and the *cheapeſt* way of cleanſing it. Tampering with fallow

fallow crops, in ſuch a caſe, is mere quackery. When land is once thoroughly cleanſed, it may, by fallow crops and due attention, be kept clean for a length of years.

But unfortunately for the occupiers of the fields which are the more immediate ſubject of theſe obſervations, they *cannot* be ſummer fallowed; *becauſe* every occupier cannot be brought into the ſame mind in any one year; conſequently, the aſſiſtance of *ſheep* cannot be conveniently had.

A Norfolk man, who has always been uſed to make his fallows with horſes only, without having perhaps a ſingle ſheep upon his farm, might well inquire if the farmers of Glóceſterſhire uſe ſheep in their plow-teams. No. But a Gloceſterſhire farmer, who has never ſeen a fallow made, which has not been at the ſame time a paſture (and ſometimes not a bad one) for ſheep, is led to believe, that a fallow cannot be made without them.—I have heard it lamented, by well meaning men, that ſuch famous land, as undoubtedly lies in theſe fields, ſhould be liable to ſuch an inconveniency. But can aſſure them, from my own practice, that, in Surrey,

Surrey, where ſimilar fields are not unfrequent, it is common to make pieces of fallow among corn; and without experiencing any material inconveniency from the abſence of ſheep, during the ſummer-ſeaſon.

If land be ſo foul as to require a whole year's fallow, it ought to have no reſpite from tillage; no time to form a ſheep paſture! Nor if through want of leiſure, or through neglect, it ſhould form one,—is it neceſſary that it ſhould be fed off with ſheep. One man we ſee plowing in a crop of turneps, buck, or vetches, worth perhaps ſome pounds an acre; while another ſuffers his land to remain in a ſtate of unproductiveneſs, leſt he ſhould plow in a few farthing's worth of ſheep feed!

The *good effect* of fallowing the "every year's land" does not ſeem to be doubted:—there is, indeed, at this time, evidence, amounting to demonſtration, in the center of one of the fields under notice. A plot, which was ſummer fallowed (by a ſuperior manager) four years ago for wheat, was this year (1788) wheat after beans. In the ſpring, and during ſummer, it diſtinguiſhed itſelf, evidently by the colour and groſſneſs of the blade; and its ſuperiority at at harveſt is not leſs manifeſt. An acre of it is worth four of ſome acres in the ſame field. (Windmill field near Gloceſter.) By obſervation ſufficiently minute, I am of opinion that, taking the reſt of the field on a par, one acre is worth two: and it is highly probable, that, with the unprecedented care, which, in this country, is taken of crops, while growing,—the effects of the fallow will be ſeen for many years henceforward.

I am of opinion that, with the practices of this country, in the ſeed and vegetating proceſſes, which will fall preſently under conſideration, a whole year's fallow *judiciouſly made* every ten, fifteen, or perhaps twenty years, would be found ſufficient to keep the land in a ſtate of cleaneſs and tilth. How extremely abſurd, then, to ſuffer them to remain in their preſent unproductive ſtate!

III. Laying up ridges. The high lands of the vale of Eveſham, have long been proverbial. Thoſe of the vale of Gloceſter are equally entitled to notoriety. It has been ſaid of them, hyperbolically, that men on horſeback, riding in the furrows, could not ſee each other over the ridges. This, we may venture

to

to ſay, was never the caſe; though heretofore, perhaps, they have been higher than they are at preſent. Not many years ago, there was an inſtance of ridges, toward the center of this vale, which were ſo high, that two men above the middle ſize, ſtanding in the furrows, could not ſee each other's heads: I have, myſelf, ſtood in the furrow of a wheat ſtubble; the tips of which, upon the ridges, roſe to the eye: a man, ſomewhat below the middle ſize, accidentally croſſing them, ſunk below the ſight in every furrow he deſcended into. But the ſtubble, in this inſtance, was not leſs than eighteen inches high. The height of ſoil from four feet to four feet three inches:—the width of theſe lands about fifteen yards.—I afterwards meaſured a furrow near four feet deep.

But an anecdote, relative to the firſt-mentioned ridges, will ſhew theſe extraordinary moments of human induſtry in a more ſtriking light, than any dimenſions which can be given. The occupier of them had, at a pinch, occaſion to borrow ſome plow-teams of his friends; one of whom called upon him, in the courſe of the day, to ſee them at work, and was directed to the field, where ſix or ſeven teams were plowing.

plowing. He went to the field (a flat inclofure of twelve or fifteen acres) but feeing nothing of the teams, he concluded he had miftaken the direction, and went back for a frefh one. The fact was, the feveral teams were making up their furrows, and were wholly hid, by the ridges, from his fight.

The width of thofe lands was twenty to twenty five yards: but lands in general are narrower, and of courfe lower; the height being, in moft cafes, nearly proportioned to the width. About eight yards wide, and two feet to two feet and a half high, feems to be, at prefent, the favourite ridge. Thefe dimenfions, though they may appear moderate upon paper, form, in the field, a fteep-fided ridge.

The ORIGIN of high ridges has long been confidered, I believe, as one of thofe fecrets, which antiquity may call its own. They are certainly monuments of human induftry; but are too *lowly* to have engaged the attention of the antiquary; and tradition, at leaft in this diftrict, is filent on the fubject.

They are not peculiar to this, but are common to moft common field diftricts, in which two crops and a fallow is the eftablifhed courfe of of husbandry. Even upon the wolds of Yorkshire, I have observed the thin light chalky loam, with which they are covered, scraped up together into high ridges.

In the vale under consideration, whose subsoil is of a nature so singularly cold and watery, there is some reason to suppose, that the soil has been thus heaped up, to render it dry and *warm*. But this could not be the motive in elevated situations, where the subsoil is absorbent. Nevertheless, we may rest assured, that they have been raised on *principle* (true or false) as they must have been raised with labour and expence.

The popular notion, here and in other places, is, that the soil was thus thrown into heaps, in order to increase the quantity of surface.

I cannot, however, think so meanly of the penetration of our ancestors, as to give in to this improbable notion. For even supposing every part of the superficies to be productive, the advantage accruing to *corn*, through such an expedient, is inconsiderable. It has no more *room to grow in* than it would have if the surface lay flat. Its roots, and its ears when formed,

formed, may gain ſome addition of freedom, but the ſtems riſe preciſely at the ſame diſtance from each other, whether the land lie flat, or is raiſed into the higheſt ridges.

But in this diſtrict, where, in winter and wet ſeaſons, each furrow, in many places, is a canal of ſtagnant water; and where, even in places in which the furrows lie above the common ſhore, ſome yards width of each is a thicket of weeds, without a blade of corn among them; the quantity of *productive ſurface* is very evidently, and very conſiderably, *leſſened.*

In every diſtrict, and in every ſituation, the ſkirts of high ridges are weak, and comparatively unproductive. For, in proportion as the ridges are raiſed, and the depth of ſoil is there increaſed, in the ſame proportion the furrows are ſunk, and the depth of ſoil there diminiſhed; the bottoms of the furrows generally dipping into a dead infertile ſubſoil.

Beſides, the ſkirts of high lands lie under another heavy diſadvantage; eſpecially where the ſoil is of a retentive nature, and the ſubſoil cold and watery: in a wet ſeaſon, after the upper parts of the lands are ſaturated, the

redundant

redundant water falls down, of courſe, to their baſes, where, meeting with a repellent ſubſoil, it is held in ſuſpence; keeping the ſkirts of the lands, ſo long as the wet ſeaſon continues, in a ſtate much too moiſt and cold for the purpoſes of vegetation.

The preſent year (1788) affords numberleſs inſtances of this evil effect. Laſt autumn was exceſſively wet. At wheat ſeed time, retentive ſoils were in a ſtate of mortar; and remained in that ſtate, until late in the ſpring. It is probable that, on the lower parts of the lands, much of the ſeed never vegetated; and the plants, which reached the ſurface, dwindled away, as the ſpring advanced. In the colder parts of the vale, the ſkirts of the lands, in the latter end of May, had the appearance of fallow-ground: in ſome particular ſituations, a ſtripe upon each ridge, only, was left: not half, perhaps not one third of the ſurface fully occupied. Whereas, had the ſame ſoil been judiciouſly laid up in narrow lands, with croſs furrows to take off the ſurface water, every foot of ſurface might have been filled, and every part been rendered equally productive.

But

But extremely difadvantageous as high ridges undoubtedly are, while they remain in a ftate of aration; they are no longer fo, when laid down to grafs. In this cafe, the furface is indifputably enlarged. Herbage, efpecially when it is paftured, fpreads every way upon the ground, and does not rife perpendicularly, as corn. Befides, in this cafe, there is a variety of herbage, and a variety of foil, fuited to every feafon. If the feafon be moift, the ridges afford a plenty of fweet pafturage, and dry ground for the pafturing ftock to reft upon: and I had an opportunity of obferving, in the year 1783, a dry year, that while the ridges, and flat lands in general, were burnt up with drought, the furrows of high lands continued in full herbage. It is obfervable, however, that in cafes, where the fubfoil is retentive, every furrow fhould have its underdrain; otherwife the herbage, efpecially in a wet feafon, will be of a very inferior quality.

The propriety of REDUCING HIGH RIDGES is a matter in difpute, among men who ftand high in their profeffion. To me there appears no room for argument. If they be intended to remain under a ftate of arable management, they ought to be lowered. On the contrary, if they be intended for a ſtate of herbage, they ought to remain in or near their preſent form: provided the furrows be ſufficiently ſound, or lie high enough for draining. If not, the ridges ought to be lowered, until the furrows be raiſed high enough to lie dry, or to admit of underdraining.

In the common fields, no attempts, I believe, have been made to lower them, in any conſiderable degree. The practice of plowing twice *upward* to once *downward*, as has been explained above, keeps them at, or nearly at, the ancient ſtandard.

There is indeed a diſadvantage attending the reduction of high ridges, which thoſe, who have had no experience in them, may not be aware of. The *cores* of the ridges; though they have been formed out of the original topſoil; which, in all human probability, was, when buried, of a ſingularly fertile nature, are now become inactive, unproductive maſſes of *dead earth*. I have obſerved, where one of theſe ridges has been cut acroſs in ſinking a ſtone pit, that the preſent ſoil forms an arch of dark-coloured rich-looking mould, a foot

to

to eighteen inches deep;—under which lies a regularly turned cylinder of ill coloured *ſub-ſoil*; reſembling the *natural* ſubſoil of the country ſo much, that, unleſs we had indiſputable evidence of theſe ridges being the work of art, we ſhould be led to conclude that nature had moulded them to their preſent form. This appears to me an intereſting circumſtance, eſpecially entitled to the agricultor's attention.

Notwithſtanding, however, this diſadvantage in reducing high ridges, I have had the opportunity of ſeeing an inſtance of practice, in which ſome of the higheſt in the diſtrict have been brought down to the deſired pitch; and, in the only way perhaps, in which the height of *arable* ridges can be decreaſed with propriety: namely that of increaſing their number.

The ſubjects, in this inſtance, were the incloſure particularly noticed in page 76; and a neighbouring incloſure; which, in 1783, was nearly reduced to the deſired ſtate. The other had, in 1783, been recently begun upon; and is now, 1788, in great forwardneſs.

The width of the lands in this caſe as has been ſaid was twenty to twenty five yards; the height five to fix feet; the furrows lying much below the furrounding ditches; fometimes holding water enough "to float a barge"!

The method of reducing them was that of gathering up a new land in each interfurrow of the old ones; which, by this means, were lowered as the intervening lands were raifed. To guard againft the difadvantage explained above, the whole of the manure which would have been fpread over the entire furface, was laid upon the crowns of the old or large lands; it being found that the new lands, being formed entirely of made-earth, were fufficiently fertile, after they got their heads above water, without the addition of manure; and the fides of the large lands were fed from the crowns, by every plowing, and every fhower. Altogether a great work, executed in a mafterly manner. *

In the open fields, where the lands lie intermixt, this method of lowering them could not be practifed. But one equally practicable is obvious: namely that of forming each large land into three; by raifing a fmall one on either fide of it. Applying the manure as in the above

* By Mr. George Piffe of Down Hatherly.

above inſtance. If a general incloſure be not near at hand, ſome of the open-field townſhips might, I ſhould imagine, reap great benefit by ſuch a reform.

On the contrary,—where an incloſure is likely to take place, and the land is naturally adapted to a ſtate of *graſs*, it might be wrong to leſſen the width of the preſent ridges. All in that caſe requiſite would be to alter their form; by reducing them from triangular *roofs* to *waves*, or ſegments of cylinders: a ſpecies of ſurface, for graſsland whoſe ſubſoil is any way inclined to retentiveneſs, which has many ECONOMICAL advantages over a flat bowling-green ſurface.

17.

MANURE.

VALE DISTRICTS, whole ſoils are generally deep and *naturally fertile*, require leſs manure than thin-ſoiled upland diſtricts; which, being *naturally infertile* (if we may be allowed to ſpeak of their original nature) require greater exertions of art, to preſerve them in a ſtate of productiveneſs.

Hence, in diſtricts of the latter deſcription, we ſee huſbandmen anxious about manure; making the moſt of that which the farm itſelf affords; fetching others from a diſtance; and ſearching beneath the ſoil for more;—while in countries covered with more generous ſoil, manures are in lower eſtimation: the degree of eſtimation varying, however, in different diſtricts of this deſcription. *

In

* The PRICE OF TOWN MANURE may be conſidered as no mean ſtandard of the ſtate of huſbandry, or at leaſt the ſpirit of huſbandmen, in the neighbourhood of the given town.

A man

In the vale under ſurvey, there is a conſiderable proportion of graſs land. That which is paſtured requires little addition of manure. And the grounds which are occaſionally mown, have ſeldom any return made them. While the meadows, being either intrinſically fertile, or liable to be overflowed, pay an annual tribute to the dung yard, without expecting any return. The arable lands, therefore, form the only object of melioration; and DUNG may be ſaid to be the only manure made uſe of in meliorating them.

MOULD is not in uſe, either in the farm yard, or at the dung heap. I have ſeen it mixed with litter, or very long dung, layer-for-layer; but this is not the common practice of the diſtrict.

MARL

A man whoſe intelligence is good, and whoſe veracity may be relied on,—has favored me with the prices of manure in the towns of this diſtrict. Gloceſter 1s. 6d. Tewkeſbury 2s. Upton and Worceſter 2s. 6d. to 3s. Eveſham 4s. to 5s. a load, of about a ton.

The comparative highneſs of the price at EVESHAM is chiefly owing to the quantity of GARDEN GROUNDS in the neighbourhood of that town; which ſupplies Birmingham, and formerly ſupplied many other diſtant markets, in a great meaſure, with garden ſtuff. There are now, it is ſaid, two or three hundred acres under the garden culture.

Marl is not common to the vale. Weakly calcarious clays are frequent. The intervening ſtrata of the ſtone of the ſubſoil are calcarious in a ſlight degree. The only earth I have found, which can with propriety be termed marl, breaks out at the ſkirts, and in the roads of the red hills of Deerhurſt; and is, I believe, common to the red lands weſt of the Severn; where it is ſaid to be uſed as a manure; and it ought to be tried, (if it has not been tried already) in the vale; though its quality appears by analyſis to be of an inferior degree; not more than one fifth of it being a pure calcarious earth.

The ſpecimen I tried was taken near Apperley. Part of it in the hollow way between the common and the village; part from the foot of the hill facing the Severn. The colour a light red, reſembling that of ſalmon-coloured bricks: the contexture inclined to ſhaley; but breaks freely in water. One hundred grains left a reſiduum of eighty grains; a cinnamon-coloured ſilt.

Lime has been tried; and, in one inſtance at leaſt, has been found very beneficial to the vale land. But I do not find that the uſe of it has

has in any instance risen into *practice*. The argument against it is, that stone is expensive to raise and coals dear. Stones at 2s. a load are certainly dear; but coals at 10s. to 12s. a ton are very cheap, compared with their price in many districts where lime is burnt for manure.

It may be laid upon the land, here, at a much easier expence than it is in Cleveland (a similar district) to which it is fetched, in the ordinary practice of husbandmen, twenty or thirty miles by land carriage. But in Cleveland the spirit of improvement has long been upon the wing: here it might be said to be still a nestling.

In the MANAGEMENT OF DUNG nothing claims particular notice; it is usually piled in the "courts" in spring; and, in the common field husbandry, carried onto the fallows the first dry season of summer. One part in the ordering of dung in this district is, however, reprehensible: if a dung hill be formed in the field, the carriages are drawn upon it; by which means its maturation is very much retarded. See NORF. ECON. vol. I. p. 158.

SEED

18.

SEED PROCESS.

IN THE SEED PROCESS, the vale farmers are above equality. Beans and peas, are almoſt univerſally SET BY HAND. Barley lands are CLODDED; and wheat "LAND-MENDED:" practices which lower, very conſiderably, the requiſite QUANTITY OF SEED. It appears to me probable, that one fourth of the quantity of ſeed, uſually ſown in moſt other diſtricts, is ſaved in this. The ſeed of barley excepted.

There is a prevailing opinion, backed by common practice, in the more central parts of the vale at leaſt, that it is dangerous *to ſow the freſh furrow of ſtiff land:* which, in this ſtate, is thought to lie "*too hollow!*" A ſtate, which the huſbandmen of the vale ſeem cautiouſly to avoid. Hence the wheat ſtubble is mown off, for beans, and the bean ſtubble drawn, for wheat; and the land ſuffered to lie ſome

ſome time between the plowing and the ſowing. Yet the lighter ſoils are ſown on the freſh furrow. In Norfolk, a lightland diſtrict, the farmers dread nothing more than their lands being cold and heavy at the time of ſowing.

Are theſe practices founded in right reaſon, or in cuſtom? If in truth,—how difficult is the theory of this part of the arable proceſs?

19.

CORN WEEDS.

THE SPECIES of CORNWEEDS, prevalent in this diſtrict, are arranged in the following liſt agreeably to their reſpective degrees of prevalency in the "every years' lands," in the neighbourhood of Gloceſter; or as nearly ſo as the intention of the arrangement requires.

The firſt ten are the moſt deſtructive.—In ſome caſes, any one of the ſpecies would be enough to deſtroy a crop, were they not checked,

checked, in the manner which will be explained. The laſt nine are naturally the inhabitants of road-ſides and hedges; but, encouraged by the plow's neglect, have ventured abroad into the fields: even the common reed I have ſeen waving its panicles, in number, over wheat, growing ſeveral lands-widths from its native ditch.

LINNEAN NAMES.	ENGLISH NAMES*:
Triticum repens,—	couch graſs.
Serratula arvenſis,—	common thiſtle.
Sinapis nigra,—	common muſtard†.
Convolvulus arvenſis,—	corn covolvulus.
Chenopodium viride,—	redjointed gooſefoot‡.
Chryſanthemum ſegetum,—	corn marigold.

Papaver

* PROVINCIAL NAMES are, in this caſe, neceſſarily omitted. The names of plants; even their provincial names; are known to a few intelligent individuals, only; no one of whom I have been fortunate enough to meet with in this diſtrict.

† COMMON MUSTARD. This is the ſpecies which is cultivated in the north of England for its flour.—It is here the moſt common weed: being, in this diſtrict, what the wild muſtard, or charlock, is in others: a circumſtance, which is leſs extraordinary than that of the diſtrict under notice being free from the latter plant. I have not been able to gather a ſingle ſpecimen in it!

‡ REDJOINTED GOOSEFOOT. This I have heard called, provincially,—" DROUGHT-WEED": an apt name for it.

Papaver Rhæas,——round ſmoothheaded poppy.

Papaver dubium,——long ſmoothheaded poppy.

Avena fatua,—wild oat*.

Equiſetum

* The WILD OAT, a plant unknown in many parts of the iſland, is here, as well as in Yorkſhire, a moſt troubleſome weed of corn. In general appearance, this plant reſembles exactly the CULTIVATED OAT: in ſtem, blade, panicle, chaff, and *kernel*, they are the *ſame* plant: and, in colour, their ſeeds are ſubject to the *ſame* varieties: namely black, red, white. But, examined botanically, the wild oat differs, in three notable particulars, from *Avena ſativa*; which i deſcribed by Linneus, as having "calyxes *two-ſeeded*; ſeeds *poliſhed*; one *awned*"; whereas the calices of the wild oat are *two or three ſeeded*; the ſeeds *covered with long ſoft hair*; and *all of them* awned. Nevertheleſs, in one inſtance, I found the lower ſeeds of the panicle *nearly ſmooth*: this, added to the circumſtance of the Poland oat (a highly cultivated variety) growing in calices *one ſeeded*, and *without any awn*, renders it much more than probable, that the various ſorts of cultivated oats are no more than CULTIVATED VARIETIES OF THE WILD OAT.

Be that as it may---the wild oat appears to be as confirmed a *native* of this iſland, as any other *arable* weed, which grows in it; and is, perhaps of all, the moſt difficult to be extirpated. It will lie a century in the ſoil, without loſing its vegetative quality. Ground, which has lain in a ſtate of graſs, time immemorial, both in this county and in Yorkſhire, has, on being broken up, produced it in abundance. It is alſo endowed with the ſame inſtinctive choice

Equisetum arvense,—corn horsetail.
Agrostis alba,—creeping bentgrass.
Alopecurus agrestis,—field foxtailgrass.
Festuca duriuscula,—hard fescue*.
Sonchus oleraceus,—common sowthistle
Artemisia vulgaris,—mugwort.
Sinapis alba,—white mustard †.
Rumex crispus,—curled dock.
Carduus lanceolatus,—spear thistle.
Galium Aparine,—cleavers.

Urtica

choice of seasons, and state of the soil, as other seeds of weeds appe r to have. This renders it, what it is considered, a difficult weed to be overcome: for ripening before any *crop*, it sheds its seed on the soil; where it probably finds safety from the birds in the roughness of its coat. FALLOWING; HOING;---and, where it is practicable, giving a final HANDWEEDING, after it shoot its panicle, are the only means of extirpation.

* HARD FESCUE. This plant, which is one of the greatest pests in the arable lands of some districts, (under the name of BLACK COUCH) is seldom met with in the plowed lands of this; notwithstanding their want of tillage: and notwithstanding it is found, (though not abundantly) in the surrounding grass lands!

† WHITE MUTARD. Its seeds in this district are *red*; some of them inclining to a dark mottle; resembling, in colour, the seeds of the cultivated vetch: none of them lighter than those of the common mustard; sinapis *nigra*; whose seeds, when in perfection, are of a bright sorrel *red*.

Urtica dioica,—common nettle.

Sinapis orientalis *.

Rumex obtuſifolius,—broadleaved dock.

Anthemis Cotula,—maithe-weed.

Matricaria ſuaveolens,—-ſweetſcented camomile.

Chryſanthemum inodorum,—weakſcented camomile.

Mentha arvenſis,—corn mint.

Centaurea Cyanus,—bluebonnet.

Polygonum Perſicaria,—common mild perſicaria.

Sonchus arvenſis,—corn ſowthiſtle.

Lapſana communis,—nipplewort.

Atriplex patula,—ſpreading orach.

Tuſſilago Farfara,—coltsfoot.

Ranunculus repens,—creeping crowfoot.

Potentilla

* SINAPIS ORIENTALIS. A plant which grows here as a troubleſome weed of corn, anſwering with great exactneſs, Linneus's deſcription of *Sinapis orientalis*, I have ventured to call it by that name; though I have not been able to find it, in any liſt of *Engliſh* plants. Its ſtature is ſimilar to that of the white muſtard; to which its general appearance has ſome affinity; but, on cloſer examination, the affinity vaniſhes. The points, with which its pods and ſtem are thickly ſet, incline *downward*; the body of the pod is *long*; and the beak *ſhort*; the ſeeds *numerous*, *ſmall*, and of a ſhining *black*.

Potentilla anſerina,—ſilverweed.
Trifolium Melilotus officinalis,—melilot.
Achillea Millefolium,—milfoil.
Stachys paluſtris,—clownsallheal.
Veronica hederifolia,—ivyleaved ſpeedwell.
Senecio vulgaris,—groundſel.
Alſine media,—chickweed.
Thlaſpi Burſa-paſtoris,—ſhepherdspurſe.
Æthuſa Cynapium,—foolsparſley †.
Ceraſtium vulgatum,—common mouſear.
Fumaria officinalis,—common fumitory.
Polygonum aviculare,—hogweed.
Plantago major,—broad plantain.
Avena elatior,—tall oatgraſs ‡.
Agroſtis capillaris,—fine bentgraſs.
Heracleum Sphondylium,—cowparſnep.
Centaurea Scabioſa,—upland knobweed.
Scabioſa arvenſis,—upland ſcabious.

Daucus

† Foolsparsley. This is here a very common field weed (a character I have not ſeen it in before) but coming late, and not riſing, in this ſituation, to a great height, its injury is little perceived.

‡ Tall oatgrass. This is another fallow-weed which is partial to particular ſoils or ſituations. Notwithſtanding the want of tillage in this diſtrict, I have not once ſeen its roots turned up by the plow.

Daucus Carota,—wild carrot.
Lychnis dioica,—common campion.
Carduus crifpus,—curled thiftle.
Lycopfis arvenfis,—corn buglos.
Lamium purpureum,—dwarf deadnettle.
Galeopfis Tetrahit,—wild hemp*.
Ranunculus arvenfis,—corn crowfoot.
Polygonum penfylvanicum,—pale perficaria.
Polygonum Convolvulus,——climbing buck-weed.
Antirrhinum Linaria,—common Snapdragon.
Hypochæris radicata,——long-rooted hawk-weed.
Euphrafia Odontites,—red eyebright.
Euphorbia Heliofcopia,—fun fpurge.

Viola

* WILD HEMP. This is another evidence of the fame fact. In Yorkfhire it ranks with the more prevailing weeds. In the midland counties it is ftill more prevalent: while here it takes place in the lower part of the catalogue.

Thefe obfervations will, I am aware, be uninterefting to the reader, who is either unacquainted with the individuals fpoken of, or is no way interefted in the nature and prevalency of corn weeds. Neverthelefs, they will, I am perfuaded, be viewed in a different light by the practical farmer, who is, at the fame time, a practical botanift; and I believe I may add, that every *good* farmer *is* a botanift, *as far as he is able*; and *ought to be*, as far as botany relates to agriculture.

Viola tricolor,—common panſie.
Prunella vulgaris,—ſelfheal.
Leont odonTaraxacum,—common dandelion.
Galium verum,—yellow bedſtraw.
Malva rotundifolia,—round-leaved mallow.
Vicia Cracca,—bluetufted vetch.
Convolvulus ſepium,—hedge convolvulus.
Galium Mollugo,—baſtard madder.
Conium maculatum,—hemlock.
Ballota nigra,—ſtinking horehound.
Eriſimum Aliaria,—garlic creſs.
Lamium album,—white deadnettle.
Arundo phragmitis,—common reed.

After what has been ſaid, under the head TILLAGE, it will be doing juſtice, only, to the vale farmers, to apprize the reader, in this place, that, inattentive as they undoubtedly are to the PREVENTION of corn weeds, they muſt not be conſidered as the avowed friends and allies of weeds: for, in the DESTRUCTION of them, they indiſputably ſtand preeminent in their profeſſion.

THE HOING OF CROPS IN GENERAL has long been held out as a thing moſt deſirable, in the arable proceſs. Here we find it nearly in full practice. Not only the ligumenous crops,

crops, which are planted in rows; but WHEAT, which is ſown at random, are hoed: not by a few individuals, only; but by huſbandmen in general: the wheat crop being hoed, here, as cuſtomarily as the the turnep crop is in Norfolk. Barley may be ſaid to be the only crop, which is not hoed. But this crop is invariably fallowed for; either by a whole year, or by a winter-and-ſpring fallow: ſo that EVERY CROP which is taken is, in reallity, a FALLOW CROP.

Hence we ſee fields which have borne crops of GRAIN, year after year without remiſſion, during time immemorial, ſtill affording annually portions of produce, which, in the management of ſome individuals, in ſome ſeaſons, may be entitled to the name of *crops*. A fact, which nothing leſs than actual obſervation, could have induced me to give full credit to. A fact which proves, in a moſt intereſting manner, the value of a due ATTENTION TO CROPS WHILE VEGETATING: a ſpecies of attention, which, in the management of the kingdom at large, is entirely omitted; excepting, perhaps, what is beſtowed on an imperfect handweeding: In general terms, it may be ſaid, that, in moſt other diſtricts, crops remain in a ſtate of neglect, from ſeed time to harveſt. While, here, the buſineſs of the arable proceſs does not appear to be ſet about in earneſt, until the crops be above ground!

The origin of this unparalleled attention to crops, WHILE VEGETATING, would now, perhaps, be difficult to trace. In all probability, it originated in a kind of neceſſity, on the every years lands; which, without it, muſt long ago have been wholly poſſeſſed by one continued thicket of weeds. Its good effect being there ſeen, it would be received, by degrees, into the fallow fields: firſt as an expedient to ſave a foul crop; and, at length, as a practice.

The excellency of this cuſtom, and the extent of its utility, are not confined to the field: the HOING OF CORN is done, chiefly, by WOMEN AND CHILDREN: induſtry is, of courſe, encouraged; and the pariſh levies probably leſſened; or, what is equally beneficial to the farmer, the wages for MEN's labour are lowered: while, in the ſaving of ſeed, by this practice, the farmer and the community are ſtill more immediately benefited.

HARVESTING.

20.

HARVESTING.

THE WORK OF HARVEST was, formerly, done chiefly by HARVEST MEN; but now, in part, by THE ACRE.

The WAGES of harveſt men are thirty ſhillings for the harveſt; or a ſhilling a-day;—with full board.

The method of VICTUALING harveſtmen, in this diſtrict, is ſingularly judicious. They have *no regular dinner.* Their breakfaſt is cold meat. Their refreſhment in the field bread and cheeſe, with ſix or eight quarts of beverage. At night, when they return home, a *hot ſupper*;—and, after it, each man a quart of ſtrong liquor; in order to alleviate the fatigues of the day which is paſt; and, by ſending him to bed in ſpirits and good humour, to prepare him for the morrow's toil.

There is more than one advantage ariſes from this cuſtom. All work within-doors, in the middle of the day, is got rid of: and the advantage of continuing the work of the field, without a break, through *the prime part of the day*, is obvious; and is highly eſtimated by thoſe who know the value of it, from experience. Converſing with an active good huſbandman on the ſubject, he exclaimed "Lord, Sir, what ſhould we do now (about noon) if we were to give our men a regular dinner! They muſt either go home to it; or we muſt bring it to them here in the field; and while they were eating, and playing under the hedge, we ſhould loſe the hauling of two or three load of beans."

The hours of work are long;—from dawn to duſk;—eſpecially when diſpatch is more particularly requiſite. The quantity of work done is above par: namely, twenty to thirty loads of corn; with one ſet of men.

21.

FARMYARD MANAGEMENT.

THE WINTER MANAGEMENT of the vale, as an *arable* diſtrict, affords nothing of excellence; nor includes any noticeable defect; excepting the prevailing one of paying too little regard to the accumulation of manure: nevertheleſs a few peculiarities require to be regiſtered.

BARN MANAGEMENT. The *method of thraſhing*, in uſe here, is that of the ſouthern counties: the ears of wheat are occaſionally lifted, and looſe corn from time to time lightened, with the ſwipple; in order to raiſe up the parts unthraſhed, and thereby expoſe them to a more effective ſtroke: a practice which is more eaſy, leſs hurtful to the grain, and perhaps not leſs expeditious, than the north-country method; in which the thraſher keeps on, with one even ſtroke, from the time the corn is ſpread upon the floor, until it be turned, or the ſtraw ſhook off.

Winnowing is here done with the ſail-fan in the ſouth-of-England manner.

Chaff is expended on cart horſes. Barley chaff is in good eſteem:—ſome farmers, at leaſt, prefer it to that of the " cone wheat" ;—a long-awned grain.

YARD MANAGEMENT. It has been already ſaid that bottoming farm yards with *mould* is not a practice of this diſtrict. They are, however, ſometimes littered with *ſtubble.*

Straw is given to cattle, looſe, in mangers and cribs of various conſtructions. (See FARM-BUILDINGS.)

It is not unuſual in the practice of this diſtrict to let ſtraw-yard cattle have a yard, foddering ground, or orchard, adjoining to the ſtraw yard, to ſtray into at pleaſure. This indulgence may be ſerviceable, perhaps, to the health of the cattle; but is certainly waſteful of manure.

22.

MARKETS.

THE PRINCIPAL MARKETS of this diſtrict, for CORN, are *Glocester* and *Tewkesbury*. *Cheltenham*, in the ſummer ſeaſon, takes off its proportion of BUTTER and POULTRY. CHEESE is bought up chiefly by *factors*; and the ſurplus of FAT CATTLE and SHEEP, after the country markets are ſupplied, goes chiefly to *Smithfield*.

MARKET PLACES never ſtruck me as a ſubject entitled to particular attention, until I ſaw the good effect which has taken place, by a reform in the market places of this diſtrict.

In 1783, the markets of Gloceſter, Tewkeſbury and Cheltenham were kept on old-faſhioned *croſſes*, and under open market-houſes, ſtanding in the middles of the main ſtreets; to the annoyance of travellers; the disfigurement of the towns; and the inconveniency of the market-people, whether ſellers or buyers.

New

Now (1788) theſe nuiſances are cleared away, and the markets removed into well ſituated receſſes, conveniently fitted up for their reception.—A ſpecies of reform which moſt market towns in the kingdom ſtand greatly in need of.

The old croſſes and market houſes are generally ſmall, inconvenient, and now no longer adequate to the purpoſes for which they were originally erected. In winter, they are chilling and dangerous to the health of thoſe who have to wait in them; eſpecially women; whoſe habits of hardineſs may not, now, be equal to what they were in the day in which theſe erections were made. Beſides, the corn-market, the ſhambles, and the women's market are frequently ſcattered in different parts of a town: while, in a ſquare incloſed with ſhops, ſhades, and penthouſes; with ſhambles in the center; and a corn market at the entrance;—the whole are brought together; rendering the buſineſs of market commodious and comfortable; epithets which, at preſent, can ſeldom be well applied to it.

In the inſtances under notice, the alterations were made by the reſpective towns; at, no

doubt,

doubt, a conſiderable expence; the intereſt of which is raiſed by tolls, payable by the ſellers: an inconveniency, which leſſens, very conſiderably, the magnitude of the improvement.

This is an intereſting ſubject, and cloſely connected with the preſent deſign. It would little avail the farmer to raiſe crops, without a market to vend them at. It is the grand center to which all his labours tend.

We may, I think, venture ſafely to ſtart as a poſition, that markets are, or ought to be made, the concerns of COUNTIES at large; not of the particular towns they happen to be kept in. They promote, indiſputably, the general benefit of towns, and the portions of country which lie immediately round them; but that of the latter more eſpecially: and it would be equally reaſonable to expect that a market town ſhould build a bridge for the country people to come over to market, as to find them ſhops to ſell their wares in.

Indeed *weekly markets* are eſſentially neceſſary, in the preſent ſtate of things, to the country; but not ſo to towns; which have markets, *daily*, in the ſhops of their own inhabitants: and that they require no weekly markets,

London

London is an inſtance. In wholeſale matters, as corn, cheeſe &c, towns have no intereſt whatever: unleſs the *inns*, as they oftentimes abſurdly are, be conſidered as the *town*: the mere *inhabitants* have none.

But although the inhabitants of *towns* have no neceſſity for a weekly market; thoſe of *villages* would find themſelves aukwardly ſituated without one. They cannot, like the town's-people, go every morning to the ſhop. One day in a week is full as much time as they can ſpare.

Nor would it be convenient to the *farmer* to depend upon the ſhopkeepers' or the huckſters' calling upon him for his produce, and giving him their own price. It is as convenient,—as neceſſary,—for farmers to go to market, as it is for merchants to go to 'change;—to learn the current price, and take their choice of buyers; as well as to meet each other, and make the requiſite bargains between themſelves.

Fairs are, in this point of view, ſtill more convenient to the farmer. How ſhould a grazier or a jobber know that he has ſtock to diſpoſe of, unleſs he had ſome means of *publiſhing* them? At the ſame time, how conveni-

ent

ent are fairs to the grazier, who can there take his choice of ſtock; as well as to the breeder, who may there make his election of price.

Towns were no doubt aware of theſe things when TOLLS were eſtabliſhed. But tolls are fetters which all fairs and markets ſhould be freed from. They interrupt the buſineſs of the day; are the cauſe of endleſs diſpute; and may, in theſe days, well be conſidered as the impoſitions of leſs liberal times, which ought to be cleared away,

Markets, more eſpecially, are a univerſal good. They bring the producer and the conſumer hand to hand. Shopkeepers and huckſters are middle men, who muſt be paid for their labour; and whatever profit they receive is ſo much loſt, either to the farmer or the conſumer.

Tolls have the ſelfsame tendency. Either the ſeller or the buyer muſt pay them; and each has his plea of complaint. The tolls of Glouceſter market are very high—almoſt exceſſive—3d. butter—2d. poultry or eggs.—The market women, of courſe, complain of the hardſhip; while the town's people are ſtill louder in their complaints; alleging that the ſellers,

ſellers, taking the advantage of the toll, charge them doubly for it. All taxes, eventually, fall on the conſumer.

This is a ſubject which has never, I believe, been agitated; but which is certainly entitled to the *higheſt* attention.

From the obſervations which are here looſely thrown together, we may venture to draw, as a concluſion, that ALL FAIRS AND MARKETS SHOULD BE FREE:

And that a REFORM in the MARKET PLACES and FAIR-STEADS* of this kingdom is wanted: not

* FAIR-STEADS in general, are ſtill leſs commodious than market places. They are moſtly confined to the *ſtreets* (barbarous uſage) and ſometimes every ſtreet in the town is a ſeparate fair-ſtead: ſo that it is impoſſible for a buyer to know what ſtock the fair conſiſts of. When a market is briſk, much of it may be ſold before he can poſſibly have an opportunity of ſeeing it. While, in other caſes, the ſtreets are ſo narrow, and the fair-ſtead ſo confined, that the value of ſtock cannot be eſtimated with ſufficient accuracy. A ſquare paddock, paled or walled round; with one gate to admit, and another to let out ſtock; the cattle being placed on the border, properly formed to receive them; and the ſheep-pens in the center, (in the manner of Smithfield market) would perhaps be found, in preference to all others, the beſt form for a fair-ſtead. How eaſily might every market town be furniſhed with ſuch a paddock.

not ſo much for the conveniency of towns, as for that of the country.

We have no ground of reaſoning, however, to expect that corporations, and lords of manors, will even give up their preſent tolls, much leſs make the requiſite reform, without ſome adequate recompence.

The COUNTIES, reſpectively, have the care of their gaols, and bridges; and it ſtrikes me, that the county-rate would be the propereſt fund for defraying the expence of a reform in their markets; and for afterward keeping in due order, fair-ſteads and market-places.

A reform in WEIGHTS and MEASURES has long been ſpoken of as a thing deſirable. It would be well if ſome GENERAL REFORM, in the fairs and markets of theſe kingdoms, could be brought about. While they remain in their preſent BARBAROUS ſtate, we cannot have full claim to the character of a CIVILIZED NATION.

WHEAT.

23.

WHEAT.

THE SPECIES of wheat, in cultivation here, are

1. "CONE WHEAT" or "BLUE CONE":—a variety of TRITICUM *turgidum*. * The ſtraw tall and reedy: the ear long, and of a duſky-purple colour: the chaff downy, with a very long awn, which falls off when fully ripe. The grain brown, tolerably well ſkinned, and of a hard flinty contexture; affording a *thirſty* flour; in good eſteem with the miller and baker. This is the prevailing wheat of the diſtrict;—whoſe produce is probably three-fourths of it of this ſpecies.

2. "LAMMAS.

* Not, however; the variety which is entitled to the diſtinction *cone*; its ears being remarkably *cylindrical*. In Northwiltſhire, I met with the TRUE CONE—or *triticum quadratum*—of Miller:—the baſe of the ear large and ſquare (hence it is there called "ſquare eared wheat") but the upper part is *conical*, tapering to a point. This variety is remarkably *turgid*;—the grains, in the baſe of the ear, burſting open the chaff, before harveſt, ſhowing themſelves plainly to the eye.

2. "LAMMAS WHEATS":—varieties of TRITICUM *hybernum*. Every thing that does not bear awns is "lammas";—which is divided into "red-ſtraw" and "white-ſtraw"—or rather into *red-chaff* and *white-chaff* lammas. Of the latter there are two entirely diſtinct ſorts; the chaff of one *ſmooth*, the other *villous*. They frequently grow together in the ſame piece, and the diſtinction probably paſſes unnoticed.

3. TRITICUM *æſtivum*,—or SPRING WHEAT: a ſpecies which has been pretty freely tried in this diſtrict; but which is not, at preſent, likely to gain an eſtabliſhment.

The CULTIVATION of wheat in this diſtrict, cannot, altogether, be offered as a model: nevertheleſs it muſt not be paſſed over in ſilence. It has one excellency, at leaſt, which entitles it to the higheſt attention.

The SUCCESION has been mentioned. *Beans*, planted and hoed, may be conſidered (except in the old fallow fields) as its common predeceſſor. *Peas* cultivated in the ſame manner, likewiſe precede it, on light land:—wheat being here grown on every ſpecies of SOIL.

The SOIL PROCESS, after pulſe, is ſometimes ſingular; and is entitled to notice. The *ſtubble* of beans is pretty generally *drawn* *; and I have ſeen, in more than one inſtance, the ſurface *breaſt-plowed*, after peas as well as beans, previous to the ſeed plowing for wheat.

This is to me a novel practice. I have not, out of this county, ſeen the breaſt plow uſed in any other intention, than that of paring off the ſurface of graſsland, in whole ſods. But the operation, in the practice under notice, is done with a very different deſign. The paring is not attempted to be turned in the nature of a ſod; the intention is merely that of ſevering the roots of weeds beneath the ſurface; in order that they may be harrowed out and deſtroyed, before the wheat be ſown. This, for the claſs of *creeping perennial weeds*, † is a ready and effectual mode of exterpation: alſo

* For *fuel*; either by the farmer; or, more generally I believe, by his labourers' wives and children; who have the fuel for their labour; a waggon being generally placed in the field to receive it, as it is drawn. Bean ſtubble plowed into the ſoil is thought to afford refuge for SNAILS; which ſometimes do the wheat crop great injury. It is alſo thought *to keep the ſoil too hollow!*

† See YORK: ECON: vol. I. p. 375.

alſo the *ſtrong-rooted*, and even the *worm-rooted* tribes are, probably, eſſentially *checked* by this practice; eſpecially as the plow, preſently afterward, makes another ſeparation at a greater depth; ſo that their feeding fibres, as well as their foliage, are to be produced afreſh.

The only objection to this practice is the expence: namely ſix or ſeven ſhillings an acre. In a country, however, where a ſingle plowing coſts more money, the expence cannot be deemed exceſſive.

But, on a ſoil free from ſtones, as the ſoils of the vale almoſt invariably are, the ſame or a ſimilar effect may be produced, in a much eaſier way. For although I had not ſeen a breaſt plow uſed in the operation; the utility and effects of the operation itſelf are familiar to me. In my own practice, in Surrey, I purſued the operation of SUB-PLOWING to, perhaps, its fartheſt limits: gaining a full view of its merits and defects. The greateſt difficulty lies in getting an implement to work, in all ſoils, and in all ſeaſons. A light wheel-plow,—with a broad ſharp ſhare, and without a mould board,—drawn by one or two horſes, is, I believe, the beſt implement which can be uſed in this operation: which, in ſome caſes, is very valuable ——See MIN. OF AGRI. dates 16 Auguſt, 10 and 20 October 1775, and 16 Auguſt 1776.

The TIME OF SOWING, November and December! If a farmer get his ſeed wheat into the ground before Chriſtmas, he is thought to finiſh in due ſeaſon. How widely different are the cuſtoms of countries, with reſpect to this important operation. Cuſtoms which are, no doubt, founded, in ſome degree at leaſt, on the experience of ages. This country is nearly a month behind the reſt of the kingdom. It is argued, by men of experience, in ſupport of this extraordinary practice, that, "late-ſown wheats are apt to be better headed"—are more productive of *grain*—than crops which are ſown more early: and the argument, duly limited, may have ſome foundation. But it is very probable, that the *peculiar* lateneſs of wheat feed time, in this diſtrict, is not eſſentially neceſſary to the natural ſituation of the vale, or to the nature of its ſoil, but ariſes, in ſome degree, out of its preſent peculiarity of management. The unproductiveneſs of the early ſown crops may be, in part, owing to the

the hoſt of weeds with which they have to encounter; while thoſe which are ſown late, eſcaping the autumnal vegetation, have fewer enemies to contend with, the enſuing ſummer.

There are two diſadvantages evidently attend late ſowing. The ſeaſon is uncertain, and the requiſite quantity of ſeed is increaſed. Much of it never vegetates, and much of that, which, if ſown in due ſeaſon, might have vegetated, falls unavoidably a prey to vermin of different kinds.

Nevertheleſs, ſuch is the ſtrength of the vale lands, and ſuch the advantages of hoing, that the QUANTITY OF SEED ſown in this diſtrict is *conſiderably leſs*, than that ſown, I believe, *in any other part of the kingdom.* Even at Chriſtmas, the quantity ſeldom exceeds *two buſhels* an acre! *Six pecks*, in September--October, would afford as full a ſufficiency of plants; and, in the more early part of the ſeaſon, *ſeven pecks, ſown broadcaſt*, is the uſual quantity of ſeed! *

 The

* SETTING WHEAT. This practice is not here in uſe; except on a ſmall ſcale. In the little encroachments round Corſe Lawn (a well ſoiled and very extenſive common-ſheep-walk weſtward of the Severn) I have obſerved ſeveral patches of wheat, planted in rows, with " ſetting pins", in the manner beans and peas are planted in this diſtrict.

The meaſure, it is true, is large: full nine gallons and a half: ſo that the ſeven pecks contain near ſeventeen gallons. But, in Norfolk, three buſhels containing near twenty five gallons, is uſually ſown, ſome weeks, perhaps, before the ſeed time commences in this country: two buſhels and a half; about twenty two gallons, may be taken as the middle quantity of ſeed wheat, throughout the kingdom.

But, in the vale of Glouceſter,—WHEAT IS UNIVERSALLY HOED: a fact which does honor to ENGLISH AGRICULTURE; and which I enter in this regiſter with more than ordinary ſatisfaction.

The hoing of wheat is one of thoſe valuable operations in huſbandry, which are leſs difficult, and more effectual, in practice than in theory. I have examined it with extraordinary attention; and ſhall beſtow upon it a minute analytical deſcription.

1. The number of hoings.
2. The times of hoing.
3. The width of the hoe.
4. The method of hoing.
5. The price.
6. The advantages.

1. THE

1. The number of hoings. Two hoings are generally ſpoken of; but are executed only in the practice of ſuperior huſbandmen. One hoing and a handweeding, however, are eſſential to good management. Two hoings, the laſt likewiſe a handweeding, might be deemed perfection. The firſt hoing, if given in due time, will unavoidably miſs many weeds, which will afterwards run up to ſeed, and foul ſucceeding crops.

Sometimes the crop is harrowed early (about the time of the firſt hoing) and hoed ſome time afterward. It is likewiſe not unfrequently harrowed preſenting after the firſt hoing: a good finiſh, which not only looſens the ſoil, and lets down a ſupply of air to the roots of the corn; but effectually diſengages the weeds from the ſoil; in which they are liable to be refixed by the feet of the hoers.

2. The times of hoing. The firſt hoing is begun in April, or as ſoon as the ſeaſon will permit. It ought to be finiſhed before the plants begin to "branch" ſtock—tiller—or make their vernal ramifications. The ſooner the ſecond hoing ſucceeds the firſt, the leſs difficulty there is in doing it; but the later

it is given, the more ſerviceable it proves; provided the crop be not immediately injured in the operation.

3. THE WIDTH OF THE HOE. It is generally underſtood, that the ſize of the hoe ought to be proportioned to the fullneſs of the crop: a thin crop requiring a wide hoe—one which is thick upon the ground, a narrow one. The narroweſt I have meaſured has been three inches; the wideſt five inches. The form is that of the turnep-hoe: except that the corners are, or ought to be, rounded off.

4. THE METHOD OF HOING. If the plants ſtand ſufficiently wide to admit the hoe between them, the entire ſurface is ſtirred. Where they ſtand cloſely, and weeds do not appear, they are paſſed over. Thus, the tops of high ridges are frequently too rank to admit the hoe, while the ſides of the lands are entirely worked over with it.

The *art* of hoing wheat is much leſs difficult than that of hoing turneps; which require a quick eye and a ſteady hand, to ſingle them out at proper diſtances: whereas, in hoing wheat, the plants, and of courſe the ſpaces between

between them, are *given*; all the hoer has to do, is to cut over the vacant patches, and draw the hoe between the plants;—length way, if the plants will admit of it; if not, and weeds intervene, to force through the end, or the corner: in doing which the plants are not much endangered; unleſs the hoe be very ſharp: for the ſame hoe, which will ſtir the ground, and cut up ſeedling weeds, will ſlip over wheat without injuring it. Wheat, rooting deep, is not eaſily eradicated; and ſhould part, or even the whole of the blades be cut off, they will, provided the crown be left, re-ſpring.

Hence WOMEN and CHILDREN may, with ſufficient ſafety, be truſted with hoes among wheat; and, where the ſoil is tolerably free from root-weeds, ſoon become ſufficiently expert.

But if couch graſs abound among wheat, which it too frequently does, not only more labour, but greater ſkill is requiſite. Couch graſs bears the ſame affinity to wheat, as the wild muſtard does to turneps; an adept will generally diſtinguiſh the plants with ſufficient readineſs, but in ſome caſes, they reſemble each

each other ſo nearly, as to be eaſily miſtaken for one another, by the inexperienced. Beſides, in this caſe the hoe is obliged to be kept with a ſharp edge; otherwiſe it will not take the couch: this, of courſe, renders it a more dangerous implement in the hands of the inadept. Therefore, under theſe diſgraceful circumſtances, men ought to be, and frequently are, on the every years lands, employed in the hoing of wheat.

This, however, does not operate againſt the general principle of HOING WHEAT BY WOMEN AND CHILDREN. No man, who has any regard for his intereſt, or to his character as a huſbandman, *attempts* to cultivate wheat in a bed of couchgraſs.

The requiſite *diſtance* between the plants, depends on the ſpecies of wheat, and the ſtate of the ſoil. Cone wheat is found to branch more than lammas.; and either of them will ſpread wider on a rich, than on an impoveriſhed ſoil. If the plants be ſtrong, ten or twelve inches is not deemed too great a diſtance.

It might, however, be wrong to ſet-out cloſe-growing plants at that diſtance: plants may

may acquire, during the autumn and winter, habits agreeable to their refpective fituations: the fingle plants to fpread,—thofe in groups to run upward; and it might be injurious, in the fpring, to place them in new fituations. Neverthelefs, it is probable that, in many cafes, the crop would be improved, if the underling plants, which rank wheat generally abounds with, were in due time removed. Crouded plants produce feeble ftraw, and puny imperfect grain: and, from the attention I have paid this fubject, I am of opinion, that a five-inch hoe might be ufed, freely, in the fulleft crop. I do not mean in fetting the plants out, fingly, like thofe of turneps; but merely in leffening their number; thereby giving thofe which were left a fufficiency of air and headroom. A turnep requires room at the root; wheat at the ear: and it is a thing of no great confequence, perhaps, whether a given fquare foot of atmofphere be filled with ears from one, two, or a greater number of roots.

5. PRICE. The ordinary price is half a crown an acre, for the firft hoing. But the requifite

requiſite labour varies with the ſtate of the crop, and the nature of the ſoil. A full clean crop, on a free ſoil, wants little labour. Nor on ſuch a ſoil, though foul with ſeed-weeds, is the labour difficult; provided the crop has not been ſuffered to run up and hide the ſurface. On the contrary, a thin tall crop, foul with couchgraſs, on a ſtubborn ſoil, in a dry ſeaſon, requires more labour than is ever paid for. I have ſeen a man hoing wheat under the laſt mentioned circumſtances, at 3s. an acre. But he barely earned day-wages; yet did not half do his work. If the ſoil be tolerably free, the ſeaſon kind, and the crop taken in a proper ſtate as to growth, notwithſtanding it may be foul with ſeed weeds, there are women who will hoe half an acre a day. Such a crop is not unfrequently done at 2s. an acre.

The ſecond hoing is frequently more tedious than the firſt; by reaſon of the crops, hiding the ground, and being in the way of the hoe.

6. The ADVANTAGES of hoing are many. The ſeed weeds are cut off; the root weeds checked; and the cruſt of the ſoil broken. By

By thus giving the roots a full ſupply of air, and the plants themſelves the full poſſeſſion of the ſurface,—they acquire a vigorous habit, and are induced to branch out, ſpread over the ſurface, and fill up every vacancy; by that means increaſing their own ſtrength, and keeping their enemies under. If a ſimile might be uſed on this occaſion, we might ſay, that the ſoil is a country contended for; the corn and the weeds contending armies:—By deſtroying, or checking the advancement of one, we give the other an opportunity of gaining full poſſeſſion.

Beſides the advantages to the growing crop, thoſe of future crops ought to be conſidered. The hoe deſtroys, in the firſt hoing, a claſs of weeds, which handweeding ſeldom, if ever ſtoops to. Indeed, before that operation uſually takes place, they are ſhrunk beneath notice: they flouriſh, however, at a critical time;—the time of branching;—and are probably the cauſe of greater miſchief, than riſes to common obſervation. The ſpecies which come moſt particularly within this claſs are the *ivyleaved ſpeedwell* or *winterweed*,—*chickweed*, and *groundſil*: while *hairough*, one of the worſt weed

weed of wheat, falls an eaſy victim to the hoe. The *ſhepherdspurſe*,--*common* and *ſcorpion mouſe-ears*, *fumitory*, *hogweed*, and other low-growing weeds, are cut off imperceptibly in HOING; but are ſeldom the objects of HANDWEEDING: conſequently, ſhed their ſeeds upon the ſoil, and remain, from year to year, a nuiſance to the growing crop.

In the HARVESTING of wheat, we find nothing particularly noticeable; except the practices of letting it ſtand until it be unreaſonably ripe,—of cutting it very high,—and of binding it in remarkably ſmall ſheaves. The laſt requires ſome attention.

The ſize of the ſheaf is here proportioned, in a great meaſure, to the height of the crop. The ſheaves being invariably bound with one length of ſtraw. The practice of making *double bands*—a practice common to the ſouthern, eaſtern, northern, and midland counties, appears to be unknown in this diſtrict. This year, the ſtraw being ſomewhat ſhort, the ſheaves (if ſuch they may be deemed) are mere handfuls—many of them may be graſped with the fingers.—Few of them are equal to half a common ſheaf; three or four of ſome of of them (eſpecially in the every years fields, where, perhaps, there are more weeds than corn to bind up) would not make a ſheaf of ſome diſtricts.

The advantages and inconveniences of this extraordinary practice require examination.

The inconveniences ariſe chiefly from the number of ſheaves. The crop takes more binding.—The trouble of band-making, however is evaded. But it is certainly more tedious to ſtook, pitch, load, unload, ſtack &c. &c. than it would be if bound in larger ſheaves; and, in theſe operations, without any obvious counter advantage.

The practice, nevertheleſs, has its advantages. Small ſheaves require leſs field room, as it is termed; that is leſs time between the cutting and the carrying; than large ſheaves do. And, what is equally valuable, if they be caught in wet weather, they are much ſooner dried again: conſequently, the danger of growing is not ſo great as when the crop is bound in large ſheaves; which frequently require opening, when a ſmall one may be got dry without that tedious and dangerous expedient.

The practices of cutting high and binding with single bands, have probably arisen, like that of hoing wheat, out of a kind of necessity on the every year's lands; on which if the weeds as well as the wheat were to be reaped, by cutting the latter low; and the whole bound up together in large sheaves;—scarcely any length of time would cure them to the center. The great length of cone wheat may have assisted in establishing the practice.

The size of sheaves, uninteresting as it may appear to those who are unpracticed in the minutiæ of husbandry, is a subject of some importance.—That the sheaves of wheat are made much too large in many districts, and perhaps in general, is as evident as that, in this district, many of them are made smaller than any good purpose can require. The difficulty lies in ascertaining the happy medium. We may venture to say, without risque, that the size ought to bear some proportion to the state of the crop. At present, it may be said to vary from a handful to an armful. How far it ought to vary, and what the proper sizes of the two extremes are, I dare not, here, take upon me to determine.

The STUBBLE and weeds are generally mown off in ſwaths, ſoon after harveſt, for litter. It is not unuſual to ſell the ſtubble on the ground. The price ſometimes ſo high as 5s. an acre; off which perhaps the buyer will carry a full waggon load! A quantity, perhaps, equal to that carried off in ſheaves at harveſt.

The PRODUCE of wheat, in this diſtrict, is below par: notwithſtanding the ſuperior quality of the ſoil. The par produce of the diſtrict is laid at *eighteen* buſhels an acre (the meaſure large). I have heard men talk gravely of *twelve* buſhels; even in the fallow fields. I have myſelf ſeen, in one of the every year's fields, not leſs perhaps than twenty, perhaps not leſs than forty acres, which could not be laid at more than *eight* buſhels an acre!

I do not mention theſe things to expoſe the huſbandmen of the vale of Gloceſter—I have no motive whatever to lead me to ſuch a conduct—nor do I, on any occaſion, I truſt, ſuffer any motive whatever to lead me to cenſure, other than the facts which appear before me. I have no partiality to this or that diſtrict. To enable me to proſecute with greater diligence the deſign I have entered upon, I endeavour to view *each* diſtrict *as my own*: and wiſh to ſee the ſeveral parcels of my wide domain; or,—in language more ſuitable to the ſubject,—the ſeveral cultivated diſtricts of this iſland, on a par as to cultivation; and as near perfection as the preſent ſtate of the art is capable of raiſing them. On the preſent occaſion, I wiſh to prove, by the moſt ſubſtantial evidence, the neceſſity of a CHANGE OF MANAGEMENT.

The diſtrict contains, without diſpute, ſome plots of cold unproductive ſoil. Every acre of it, which lies out of the water's way, may nevertheleſs be ſaid to be WHEAT LAND. Three fourths of it is land of ſuch a quality that it ought never to be ſown with wheat, without a fair probability of THREE TO FOUR QUARTERS AN ACRE. The preſent unproductiveneſs is a loſs to the community; and reflects equal diſgrace on its owner and its occupiers.

There muſt be ſome cauſe or cauſes of this ſtriking deficiency of produce; and it behoves the landowners to aſcertain and remove them: their intereſt is the moſt materially concerned.

If

If the deficiency be owing to the open fields being worn down by arable crops, (which I believe is one very great caufe of it)—why let them remain in their prefent unprofitable ftate? Why not inclofe them, and let the lands be laid to grafs?

If the deficiency be caufed by the land's being chilled with furface water (as much of the central parts of the vale undoubtedly is) why not obtain an act of fhores: and under it keep them, as they may undoubtedly be kept, fufficiently free from it.

If the coldnefs of the fubfoil be the caufe, (as it may be in fome places) encourage underdraining.

If, on examination, the caufe of a deficiency of produce fhould appear to be principally owing to a deficiency of tillage (as in the every year's lands it affuredly is)—give due encouragement to fallowing; and check, by every other poffible means, the prefent difgraceful practice of growing eight bufhels of wheat an acre, on land which is by nature enabled to bear four times that quantity.

The reform which is here offered is wanted in various other diftricts of the kingdom; in which the wheat crop, by injudicious management, is too frequently difgraceful to Englifh hufbandry. The wheat crop, above all others, fhould not be *rifqued*. No man ought to fow wheat where he has not, with a common feafon, a moral certainty of a crop.

24.

BARLEY.

THE QUANTITY of barley grown in this vale is very confiderable. For, notwithftanding the uncommon *coldnefs* of much of the vale lands, this is the only fpring *corn* which is cultivated on them.

The only SPECIES that I have feen cultivated in the diftrict is the common LONG-EARED BARLEY: HORDEUM *zeocriton*.

In the CULTIVATION of barley, one circumftance, only, is noticeable: namely that of its being made ufe of, on the every year's lands, as the *cleanfing crop*.

It

It appears to be a leading article of faith, among the occupiers of theſe lands, that if a week or ten days fine weather, in the ſpring, can be had for the operation of harrowing out couch; and if, after this, a full crop of barley ſucceed; eſpecially if it ſhould be fortunate enough to take a reclining poſture; the buſineſs of *fallowing* is effectually done:—the ſoil being thus raiſed to a degree of cleanneſs and tilth ſufficient to laſt it through a ſeries of ſucceeding crops.

Hence, to catch a few fine days to fallow in, barley is ſown, on theſe lands, very late:—the middle of May—ſometimes the latter end of May—ſometimes the beginning of June—this year (an aukward ſeaſon) barley was ſown towards the middle of June.—And, to obtain a full crop, three to four buſhels an acre is invariably ſown; under the idea that a full crop of barley, eſpecially if it lodge, ſmoothers all ſorts of weeds; even couch graſs itſelf. And true it is, that under lodged barley the ſoil grows mellow, and weeds get *weak*.

Nevertheleſs, I mean not to recommend a practice which is already too prevalent; not in this diſtrict, only, but in others: where we ſee men catching at a barley fallow, as a twig which will keep their corn above the weeds a few crops longer. The conſequence is, the barley crop, by being ſown out of ſeaſon, is of an inferior value, and ſucceeding crops, by having a hoſt of weeds to ſtruggle with, are rendered equally unproductive.

If the land be tolerably clean, and the ſeaſon favourable, a barley fallow may no doubt be of eſſential ſervice. But there is not one year in five, in which, even land which is tolerably clean, can be ſown in ſeaſon and at the ſame time be much benefitted by it for future crops.

I am well aware that even land which is foul with couchgraſs, may, by harrowing, raking and handpicking, at an unlimited expence, and ſowing the barley ſome weeks behind its time, be made to appear, to the eye, perfectly clean at barley ſeed time; but whoever will examine it after harveſt, or the enſuing ſpring, and compare its ſtate then, with that of land which has had a turnep or a whole year's fallow, will ſcarcely beſtow the labour of harrowing, and raking,

and

and picking; and riſque the loſs of his barley crop, a ſecond time. *

I have ſaid the more on this ſubject, becauſe it is an important one. I know no practice ſo popular, and at the ſame time ſo deſtructive of good huſbandry, as that of tantalizing foul land with a barley fallow. And I offer my ſentiments upon it, in this place, becauſe I hope I ſhall never have a more ſuitable opportunity.

Barley is HARVESTED looſe: mown with the naked ſithe; lies in ſwath till the day of carrying; and is cocked with common hay forks.

The MARKETS for barley are Gloceſter and Tewkeſbury. The buyers, malſters of the diſtrict, and factors who buy for the Briſtol brewers.

The PRODUCE, on a par, three quarters an acre: the meaſure very large.

* I ſpeak, here, of land which is kept under a courſe of arable crops; rather than of that which is occaſionally broken up from graſs, and laid down again, when two or three crops of corn have been taken: a practice which I may have occaſion to ſpeak of fully, in another place.

The QUALITY of the vale barley is ſuch as recommends it to the malſter, in preference to hill barley that affords a more ſightly ſample. But there ſeems to be a quality in the ſoils of theſe vales which gives ſtrength and richneſs to every article of their produce.

25.

OATS.

OATS, it has been ſaid, are not a produce of this diſtrict; at leaſt none of the CULTIVATED varieties are: the WILD OAT grows every where with unuſual ſtrength and productiveneſs.— Many laſts of it are, every year, no doubt produced.

I have never however yet ſeen a low-ſituated, ſtrong-ſoiled, cold-bottomed country, which has not been found, on experience, to be better adapted to oats than to barley. And I have not, in this diſtrict, met with any experience, or indeed with any reaſoning, which attempts

tempts to prove the contrary. Cuſtom alone is pleaded. *

This excluſion of the oat crop from the lands of the vale,—extraordinary as it appears at firſt ſight,—may perhaps be accounted for in this way. The monks preferred ale to oaten cake; barley of courſe became the favorite crop: the monaſteries were numerous: the lighter lands were not adequate to the demand:—the barley crop, therefore, was neceſſarily extended to the ſtrong lands. The monaſteries, it is true, have long been diſſolved; but the ſpirit of improvement

* Since writing this article, I have received, (from very reſpectable authority) in anſwer to a query on this ſubject, that " the vale land is natural to oats; which, if once ſown and ſhed their ſeed, will remain in the land for ever;" that is, will become a weed to future crops: and further, that under this idea, " few oats are given, in the vale of Eveſham to farm horſes (uſing beans in their ſtead) as they are ſuppoſed to paſs through them in a vegetative ſtate." Theſe fears, however, appear, to me, to be groundleſs. I have not, in any diſtrict, found the *cultivated oat* lie longer than one winter in the land: nor have I, in this diſtrict, found a *cultivated oat* in the character of a weed: for although I have diſcovered ſome few individuals with the grains of the lower part of the panicle, nearly ſmooth; yet the upper parts of the panicle have always evinced them, plainly enough, to be the *genuine wild oat*: the NATURAL SPECIES.

provement (excepting a partial reform which has lately taken place in ſome of the fallow fields) has ſlept ever ſince. The preſent ſyſtem of management (of the arable land at leaſt) was probably formed under the influence of the monaſteries; and has fallen thro' ſucceeding generations, without receiving any material change.

This, however, by the way. I do not mean to cenſure the vale huſbandmen for not ſowing oats, in preference to barley. I have had no opportunity of comparing their produce. Nevertheleſs, I would wiſh to recommend a trial of oats, on the ſtronger colder lands, in the area of the vale. Theſe lands can ſeldom be got ſufficiently fine for barley. Much ſeed muſt every year be buried in them. I have ſeen barley ſown over a ſurface on which ſome men would have been afraid to truſt oats. The clotting beetle, it is true, fines the immediate ſurface, and gives relief to many grains which lie near it: nevertheleſs thoſe which fall down the deeper fiſſures muſt, in the tender nature of ſeedling barley, be irretrievably loſt.

On

On the contrary, oats might, almoſt in any year, be ſown without hazard or difficulty; and, in the fallow fields, might be got in ſoon enough to break up the fallows, without ſix or ſeven horſes to one plow. Beſides, in a dairy country, the fodder from oats, if the ſort were well choſen, would be found of much more value—more of it—and of a better quality—than that of barley. While the produce of grain,—if theory and compariſon may in any caſe be truſted,—would more than over-ballance, in quantity, the comparative difference, in price: more eſpecially as oats would be a crop new to the vale land. See YORK: ECON: vol: II. p. 21.

PULSE.

26.

PULSE.

AT length we have paſſed the ground of cenſure; and are now entering on a ſubject of praiſe, to which it will be difficult to do juſtice: ſo *mixed* is the management of this intereſting diſtrict. Its cultivators might be called, without incurring a paradox, THE BEST AND THE WORST FARMERS IN THE KINGDOM. Were they as attentive to the SOIL, in freeing it from *ſuperfluous water*, and from the *roots* and *ſeeds* of weeds, as they are in freeing the CROPS from the *herbage* of weeds—they might well be ſtyled the firſt huſbandmen in Europe.

PULSE, whether BEANS or PEAS, ſeparate or mixed, are, in the ordinary practice of the diſtrict, PLANTED BY WOMEN, and HOED BY WOMEN AND CHILDREN, once, twice, and ſometimes thrice; giving the crop, when the ſoil is ſufficiently free from root weeds, a gardenly appearance, which is beautiful to look on, in the

the former part of the summer; and which, at harvest, if the season prove favorable, seldom fails of affording the cultivator more substantial gratification: while the soil, under this practice duly performed, is left in a state extremely well adapted to future crops; particularly the wheat crop.

The SPECIES of pulse in cultivation, here, are

1. BEANS—the large hog-bean: a variety of VICIA *faba*.

2. GREY PEAS; and

3. WHITE PEAS: varieties of VICIA *pisa*.

4. PEABEANS; namely a mixture of beans and grey peas; in various proportions. Generally, a few peas among a large proportion of beans: I have however seen, on the lighter lands, a few beans among peas; by way, I suppose, of natural rods to the crop.

The CULTIVATION of pulse in this district requires to be registered in detail.

I. SUCCESSION. Pulse succeeds invariably a corn crop: namely, wheat in the old fallow field course; barley in the new;—either wheat or barley on the every year's lands.

SOIL

II. Soil. Every ſpecies. The ſtronger ſoils beans, or beans and peas mixed;—the middle ſoils generally the ſame; the lighter ſoils in the neighbourhoods of Glooceſter and Cheltenham, peas, of various ſorts. But, in the area of the vale, few peas are grown; except among beans; which are, throughout, the prevailing crop; and which, alone, are entitled to particular attention.

III. Tillage. Begin plowing as ſoon after Chriſtmas as the ſeaſon will permit; fetching up the ſoil as deep as the plow will turn it:—nine, ten or more inches deep; and let it lie in whole furrow "to take the froſt."

IV. Manure. The bean crop, in the common practice of the diſtrict, is ſeldom manured for.

V. Seed process. This will require to be particularized.

1. The time of setting. Begin about Candlemas; or as ſoon after that time as the land can be got upon with the harrows, to break the plits and level the ſurface for the ſetters. The ſoils of this vale are moſtly of ſuch a nature that, after being frozen, they fall like lime; once going over with the harrows being

being on the colder ſoils ſufficient to reduce the ſurface to powder as fine as aſhes ; leaving not the trace of a whole furrow.

2. The METHOD OF SETTING varies in different parts of the diſtrict. In the central and ſouthern quarters, the prevailing practice is to ſet *acroſs* the ridges, *by the eye*, without a line! About Cheltenham and along the northern border, it is a practice, equally prevalent, to ſet *lengthway* of the ridges, *by a line*. While about Tewkeſbury, and towards Deerhurſt, it is common to ſet *by a line*, *acroſs* the ridges.

In theory, a *line* appears to be neceſſary. In practice, however, it is otherwiſe. Women, who have been long in the habit of ſetting without one, are able to go on, pretty regularly, by the eye alone; and the young ones are trained up, by putting one of them between two who are experienced. Upon the whole, however, a line appears to have its uſes. The ſoil becomes, in all probability, more evenly occupied by the roots; and the plants are ſomewhat more conveniently hoed;—when the ſeed is planted in ſtraight lines, with equidiſtant intervals.

Each

Each ſetter is furniſhed with a "ſetting pin," and a "tuckin;" namely, a ſatchel (hung before, by a ſtring round the waiſt) to carry the beans in. The *ſetting pin* reſembles the gardener's dibble: with, in general, however, a valuable improvement: a croſs pin, or half crutch, near the top, to reſt the palm upon; with a groove on each ſide of the main pin to receive the forefinger and the thumb. The length of the dibble (which is about two inches ſquare in the middle tapering conically, to a ſharp point) is about eight inches; of the handle, about four.

In *ſetting*, the women walk ſideway, to the right; with their faces toward the ground which is ſet: the laſt row, therefore, is immediately under the eye, and the difficulty of ſetting another row, nearly parallel with it, is readily overcome by practice. An expert hand will ſet with almoſt inconceivable rapidity.

The *diſtance* between the rows varies from ten to fourteen inches. Twelve inches may be conſidered as the prevailing width throughout the diſtrict. The diſtance, in the rows, about two inches; making the holes as cloſe

as

as can well be done, without their interfering with each other;—and about two inches deep; dropping one bean in each hole*.

3. The QUANTITY OF SEED—from two and a half to three bushels an acre.

4. The PRICE OF SETTING—-sixteen to eighteen pence a bushel: costing from 3s. 6d. to 4s. 6d. an acre.

The practice of setting *by the bushel*, appears to be, in one particular at least, very injudicious. Instead of a single bean being assigned to each hole, two and sometimes more, are put in;—that the bushel may be sooner emptied: for the same purpose, and with the same dishonest intention, a handful will not unfrequently be thrust into a hole, and covered up with mould. The only danger, in setting *by the acre*, would be that of the seed's being put in

* In the Cheltenham quarter of the district, I have observed a singular method of setting *peas*;—not in continued lines; but in clumps; making the holes eight or ten inches from each other; putting a number of peas in each hole. This is called "bunshing" them. The hoe has, undoubtedly, in this case, greater freedom: all the danger arising from the practice is, that the soil is not so evenly and fully occupied by the roots in this case, as they are when the plants are distributed in continued lines.

in too thin. But it being a notorious fact, that beans, which stand thin, are (under the same circumstances) invariably better podded, than those, which stand in a close crouded state;—it is highly probable that, of the two evils, setting by the acre would be found the least.

5. The COVERING is generally done with tined harrows, drawn once in a place. If, however, the soil be in so light, so floury a state, that the tines pull up the beans, a thorn harrow is generally made use of for the purpose of covering the seed.

VI. VEGETATING PROCESS. Presently after the beans are above ground, the surface is sometimes loosened with the HARROW; previous to the HOING.

TIME OF HOING. The first hoing is given as soon as the plants are free from the danger of being buried by the hoe. They ought, if the weather permit, to be begun upon, before they be a hand high.

The METHOD OF HOING is the common one, which is practised by gardeners, in hoing drilled crops. The intervals are cut-over, as close to the plants as can be done with safety: and, if a gap or vacancy occur in the row, the

the hoe is drawnthrough it: the hoer taking two, and ſometimes three intervals at once.

The WIDTH OF THE HOE for beans, I believe, is invariably five inches. In this caſe, the corners may be kept on, and the edge kept ſharp, with little fear of injury.

The SECOND HOING is, or ought to be, deferred as long as it can be with ſafety. It is, however, or ought to be, always finiſhed before the beans begin to blow: it being conſidered very injurious to the crop, to hoe it when the "blows are on."

The ſecond hoing is ſtill *flat*,—as the firſt. I have not ſeen an inſtance in this diſtrict, of beans being earthed up.

In the ſecond hoing, the rows are, or ought to be, carefully HAND-WEEDED. Not a weed ſhould be left ſtanding. Beans cannot blow among weeds: and every one now left, furniſhes the ſoil with a freſh ſupply of ſeeds for the annoyance of future crops.

GENERAL OBSERVATIONS ON HOING. The ſecond hoing is eſſentially neceſſary to common good management. Without it, the firſt is of little avail: it may looſen the ſoil, and give a temporary relief to the young plants; but the number of weeds, *at harveſt*, will be nearly the ſame, as if it were not to take place; for though, no doubt, it deſtroys numbers, it unlocks the ſeeds of others, which riſe up in their ſtead,—high enough to injure the growing crop; and to give a ſupply of ſeeds to the ſoil.

Weeds injure beans, and all pulſe, in a way, in which they have it not in their power to hurt corn. Corn bears its ſeed on the ſummit of its ſtem. The weeds muſt be aſpiring, indeed, if it cannot blow in defiance of them. Nor, during the maturation, is the grain (in ordinary caſes) liable to be over-ſhaddowed and crouded by weeds. On the contrary, beans throw out their ſeed from the ſides of the ſtems; down to within a few inches of the ground; provided they have room, air, and ſun enough to encourage them to throw out bloſſoms, and to enable them to bring the pods to due perfection. And it is obſervable, that a crop of beans ſeldom turns out productive, unleſs the pods form low on the ſtems.

Hence the utility of the firſt hoing;—to prevent the weeds from crouding the beans; and thereby give them a tendency to run upward;

as

as well as prevent them effectually from forming the neceſſary rudiments below: and of the ſecond;—to give the beans an opportunity of blowing; as well as of maturing their pods without the interference of weeds.

Hence, likewiſe, the unproductiveneſs of a thick-ſtanding rank crop; which, by drawing up the individuals, tall and ſlender, forms a ſhade below, and prevents a due circulation of air; the plants, in this caſe, operating as weeds to each other. And hence the uſe of THINNING a rank crop of beans, whenever they ſhow a tendency to draw each other up tall and "rammelly;"—a ſpecies of crop, which, it is well underſtood in this diſtrict, fills the rick-yard, but not the granary*.

The PRICE OF HOING, is generally ſix ſhillings an acre, for the two hoings and the "handpulling;"—more or leſs, according to the nature of the ſoil, the height of the crop, and its degree of foulneſs †.

 6. HAR-

* TOPPING, if done in due ſeaſon, aſſiſts in the ſame intention.

† The HORSE HOING of beans is not in any degree of practice; the only inſtance of deviation from the common practice of handhoing, was one, in which an ASS was made uſe

VII. Harvesting. The method of harvesting varies with the length of the crop.

A short low-podded crop is necessarily mown;—usually with a naked sithe;—letting the plants drop upon their roots. Having lain some time to wither, in this scattered state, they are gathered, with common forks, into swath-like rows, on the sides of the lands: where, having lain a further time, proportioned to their ripeness, their weediness, and the state of the weather, they are made up into wads or bundles, with the same implement, and set upon the ridges of the lands; and there remain, in that state, until they be fit for hauling. If the crop be stouter, it is sometimes bound after the sithe, and dried in shuck.

But tall beans are usually cut with a reaping hook, and a hooked stick; with which, instead of the hand, they are gathered.

Reaping beans. The larger end, or handle, of the *gathering hook* is eighteen inches long

use of in this operation! Seeing the smallness of the feet, and the narrowness of the tread of this animal, it appears to be singularly adapted, on free light soils, to the operation.

long, the ſhorter end, or hook, twelve inches; its point ſtanding out about twelve inches from the handle. The *reaping hook* in this operation, is uſed in a ſingular way; *ſtriking* with it beneath the gathering hook; making a ſweep as with a ſithe; driving the cut beans forward, until about half a moderate ſheaf be collected.

In this caſe, they are left awhile to wither in open reaps, and are afterward either bound in ſheaves and ſet up in ſtooks; or, much more uſually, are ſet up in what are termed "HACKLES:"—ſinglets of unuſual ſize; and of a conſtruction ſufficiently ſingular to merit deſcription.

The reaps are generally gathered up by two boys; who, taking them in their arms, ſingly, adjuſt their butts; by letting them fall upon them; thereby giving a level even baſe. Three or four of theſe reaps (about half a ſheaf each) are ſet up in a hollow cone-like form; as flax is ſometimes ſet up after being rated; or as hop poles are ſometimes piled. A man follows, and ties a band, made of three or four bean ſtems—a length of peaſ-halm, or a twiſted rope of long graſs,—near the top of the hackle, as it ftands: and, to fecure it ftill more from the wind, as well as to prevent its yet leafy broom-like top from catching driving fhowers, and conveying the rain water down into the body of the hackle, —he draws a fingle ftem from the middle of it, until only a few inches of its butt remain; or enters one which he finds loofe, a fimilar depth: then, taking the whole top in his hand, with the long ftem in the center of it, twifts it round in a fpiral manner; thus making the hackle a perfect cone; its apex refembling the point of a fnail-fhell; and fixes it in this form, by winding the fingle ftem round the top; burying its end within the hackle.

The crop remains in this ftate, until it be taken up by the carriages;—the *Glocefterfhire hackle* not being rebound, like the *Yorkfhire gait*, previous to the carrying; the band and the twift at the top hold them together, until they be got onto the waggon, at leaft.

In "*hauling*," it is cuftomary for boys or others (employed by the farmer) to pick up the fcattered beans, by hand, after the waggon.

VIII. In the center of the vale, BEAN HALM is thrown into the horfe rack, and the offal ftrewed about the yard as litter. About Glocefter, great quantities of it (as well as fome ftraw) are bought up at a potafh manufactory, and burnt for the afhes!

IX. The MARKETS for beans are the market towns of the diftrict; at which they are bought for horfes and for hogs, (of which they are here a principal article of fatting:) and Briftol; whofe factors buy up great quantities for the inns; (beans being throughout this divifion of the kingdom ftill ufed as a provender of horfes) and for the Guinea fhips; as food for the negroes, in their paffage from Africa to the Weft Indies.

X. The PRODUCE of beans, on a par of years and crops, is about three quarters an acre. Four quarters—that is, about thirty eight Winchefter bufhels, are not a very extraordinary crop: though much of the land which produces them has borne beans every 3d year, and fome of it, perhaps, every fecond year, during a fucceffion of ages. Something may be due to management, and much to the nature of this plant; which appears to flourifh, flouriſh, unabatingly, on ſtrong, deep land. The reſt may be owing to the natural richneſs and peculiar depth of the vale ſoils.—Beans ſtrike deep, and probably feed, in ſome meaſure at leaſt, beneath the ordinary paſture of plants.

27.

CULTIVATED GRASSES.

IN A COUNTRY, whoſe lands lie chiefly in common arable field, or in old graſs incloſures,—the CULTIVATION OF GRASSES, either as *temporary* or as *perennial* ley, is, of courſe, confined within narrow limits: nevertheleſs, the two ſpecies of cultivation require to be noticed in this place.

I. TEMPORARY LEY. Paſture lands are too abundant, and hay too cheap, to require much temporary ley to be made. In the improved courſe of the fallow-field land, ſmall pieces are, however, not unfrequently ſown with CLOVER (common red clover) inſtead of beans;

beans; by way of *green herbage* for farm-horses; and sometimes larger pieces; for *seed clover.*

The quantity of CLOVER HERBAGE, which some of the vale lands throw out, is extraordinary. The lighter lands are thought to be "too free for clover!" Running it too much to *halm*; which trails upon the ground like that of peas! It will not, it is said, answer on this soil, either for soiling or for seed; for if mown, even twice, the third crop will be rotten before the seed be ripe!

But the stronger lands produce a more upright clover-like crop;—generally, however, of uncommon luxuriance. It is usually mown, as green herbage, three times in the course of the summer. If made into hay, the quality is found to be extremely good. If cut in due season, and properly made, it is thought to be equal to meadow hay, as an article of fatting for oxen.

Such is the value of the CLOVER CROP on *fresh lands,*—on lands which are new to it: and such, we may fairly add, is the *natural strength* of the lands of this district. How truly absurd, then, to suffer the common fields

fields to remain in their prefent unproductive ftate. Not clover, only, but every other fpecies of CULTIVATED HERBAGE, adapted to the feveral foils, would, no doubt, be productive.

In the fame unprofitable ftate lay the lands of the vale of Pickering*. They had borne *grain* until they would barely pay for the labour of cultivation. The yeomanry ftarved on their own lands. They were not worth, as arable lands, 10s. an acre. But, having been inclofed and kept in a ftate of *herbage*, they now, many of them let from 30 to 40s. an acre.

It muft be allowed, that fome confiderable expence attends the inclofure of open lands; and that it is fome years before the herbage arrives at its moft profitable ftate. In the cafe here inftanced, the land lay feveral years nearly in a ftate of wafte †. But it does not follow, that, in thefe more enlightened days, the fame method of leying fhould be practiced. They might, now, on a certainty, be rendered

* See YORK. ECON. I. 291.

† See YORK. ECON. II. 84.

rendered productive from the day of inclosure. But of this in the next section.

In the management of SEED CLOVER, I have met with nothing worthy of notice; except the practice of thrashing it in frosty weather: or rather the idea of giving the preference to such weather for thrashing it in. The advantage is evident, when the idea is known; but it does not seem to have struck universally: I therefore give it a place in this register.

II. PERENNIAL LEYS. The recent attempts at laying down arable land to grass, in this district, have been made principally on the lands mentioned aforegoing, as being broken up from a state of rough pasture, and sown repeatedly with wheat (see page 67.)—But these attempts, I believe, have generally been unsuccessful. The soil reduced to a state of foulness, by repeatedly cropping it on single plowings, had no other cleansing, perhaps, than a barley fallow; and, in this foul state, was probably rendered still fouler, by sowing over it the seeds of weeds, under the name of "hay seeds."—No wonder that land laid down to grass, in this manner, should,

in

in a few years, require to be given up again to corn.

Hay seeds, however, is an indefinite term. Seeds collected from known hay, of a well herbaged ground, cut young, ſhook or thraſhed upon a floor, and ſifted through fine ſieves, to take out the large ſeeds of weeds, with which all old graſslands abound, might be eligible enough; provided ſtill purer ſeeds could not be had. But what is generally thrown upon land, under the denomination of "hay ſeeds," is a collection of the ſeeds of the ranker weeds, with few or none of thoſe of the finer graſſes.

One of the fineſt graſs grounds, I have ſeen in the vale, was laid down with hay ſeeds, about five and twenty years ago; but it was with ſeeds of the former deſcription; and the management in every other reſpect equally judicious. The land had been in bad hands, and was become extremely foul with couch; it was, therefore, ſummer fallowed. But the ſeaſon proving unfavourable, it was deemed, the enſuing ſpring, not yet ſufficiently clean. It had, therefore, a ſecond year's fallow!—By repeated plowings and harrowings, acroſs the

the ridges, they were pulled down from from roofs to waves. The next enſuing ſpring, it was ſown with barley and hay ſeeds: the moſt *ſpirited* inſtance of practice, I have met with in this moſt important branch of rural economics. And the event proves its eligibility in a ſtriking manner. Before this two year's fallow, the land let for 10s. an acre: foul as it was, at the time it was broken up, no crop could grow in it; it was worth nothing to the occupier for one year. It is now worth from 25 to 30s. an acre.

On the other hand, I have had opportunities of obſerving ſeveral inſtances of lands, which have been laid down with "hay ſeeds," and which, at preſent, lie a diſgrace to Engliſh agriculture. This ſpring I lifted the plants of a piece laid down in this diſgraceful manner.

In *May*, the only *graſs* was the bromegraſs—(oat graſs—loggerheads—lob.) and of this but a very ſmall quantity. The *weeds* were as follow: *corn horſetail,—broad plantain,—common thiſtle,—groundſel,—crowfoots,—convolvulus,—docks,* &c. &c. Half the ſurface was actually bare: no appearance of a quarter

quarter of a crop; even of weeds. In *September*,—I found it over-run with the *ox-tongue* (*picris echioides*) whoſe ſeeds were blowing about, to the annoyance of the neighbourhood. And this, I am afraid, may be taken as a ſpecimen of the preſent method of laying land down to *graſs*, in the vale of Glocеſter.

The only reaſon given for perſevering in this unpardonable practice is, that no better ſeeds are to be had; RAYGRASS being "ruinous to the vale lands"!—"Smothering every thing: and impoveriſhing the ſoil, until it will grow nothing"!

In the next article, it will appear, by the catalogues there given, that the predominant herbage of the old graſs lands of the vale is RAYGRASS. But leſt the general account which will there be given of the graſſes ſhould not be thought ſufficiently concluſive, I will here copy a ſeries of memoranda, made on the ſubject, in the autumn of 1783: before I became acquainted with the rooted antipathy, which I have ſince found to be formed, againſt raygraſs.

"*Hatherley*, 10 *Sept*: 1783. Obſerving in a ſmall incloſure, which has been lately laid down

down (or more accurately ſpeaking is laying itſelf down) to graſs, ſome green ſwardy patches beginning to make their appearance through a carpet of couch and other foulneſs, I examined the ſpecies which were thus employed in rendering the land, in deſpite of bad management, uſeful to the occupier; and found them to conſiſt wholly of raygraſs and white clover. This led me to a more minute examination of the adjoining ground, eſteemed the beſt piece of graſsland in the neighbourhood, and, from the ſeed ſtems which are now remaining in the ſtale patches, I find the bladegraſs to be chiefly raygraſs, with ſome dogstail, and a little ſoftgraſs."

"*Sept:* 11. In my ſtroll this morning, in the center of the vale, I met with an extenſive ſuite of cow-grounds (by the ſide of the Chelt in Boddington) the ſoil five or ſix feet deep. The herbage white clover and raygraſs: the young ſhoots of the raygraſs as ſweet as ſugar! Much ſweeter than any I have before examined. Theſe grounds (late Long's) are, it ſeems, very good ones for grazing; but are difficult to make cheeſe from."

"I have no longer a doubt about the herbage of church ground confifting *at prefent* (the middle of Sept.) in a manner wholly of ray grafs and white clover; for in my walk this evening, I carefully examined feveral plants of raygrafs, which had both feedftems and blades belonging to them; and, on examining the blades with a glafs, and comparing them with the turf of this field, I find they are identically the fame. In *tafte*, however, the different fpecimens vary confiderably; and *perhaps* the tafte of raygrafs might be taken as a criterion of foils; and *perhaps*, with the affiftance of a glafs, not only this but any other grafs may be known, with certainty, by the blade alone."

"*Sept:* 15. Tewkefbury lodge, a charming grafsland farm: a bold fwell covered with a rich warm foil, occupied by a luxuriant herbage; chiefly raygrafs! Some white clover; and fome other of the finer bladegraffes. "All green": not a foot of plowed land!"

"Below Apperley,—an extenfive whole year's common, ftocked with horfes, young cattle, fheep and geefe: the fite a dead level, fubject to be overflowed; the foil a redifh loam; the herbage raygrafs—(faccharine in a fuperior degree—literally as fweet as fugar!)—

with

with ſome white clover, and from what I can judge by its growth, ſome marſh bent. It is eaten down ſo level and ſo bare, that the geeſe, one would ſuppoſe, could ſcarcely get a mouthfull; yet the young cattle are as ſleek as moles: it is eſteemed, I underſtand, without exception, the beſt piece of land in the country."

In proof, however, of raygraſs being wholly unfit for the vale lands, I have been ſhown a piece which was laid down with "ryegraſs:" and, certainly, a more ſhameful piece of ley was never ſhown. Perceiving, however, from the rubbiſh upon it, that the ſeeds of rubbiſh, not thoſe of raygraſs, muſt have been ſown, I made enquiry into the complection of the ſeed, and found that it was bromegraſs--lob--loggerheads--fetched from the hills, where that graſs abounds, which had "ſmothered every thing" (even the ray graſs which might have been ſown among it) except a few of the ranker weeds. And ſimilar evidences of the ruinous nature of "rye graſs" I have met with in other diſtricts.

The bromegraſs and other weeds, which have been ſown hitherto under the name of rye graſs, are certainly improper for the vale ſoils;

ſoils ; and it is poſſible that even the *variety* of *real* raygraſs which is cultivated may not be eligible. In Yorkſhire, I found a variety (in a garden) which had evidently a *couchy* habit.

But how eaſy to collect the NATIVE SPECIES, which abounds on the old graſslands ; and thus raiſe a new variety, adapted, on a certainty, to the vale land. The difficulty of doing it would vaniſh the moment it were ſet about: it only wants a little exertion: a ſmall ſhare of indolence to be ſhook off.

If *real* raygraſs has ever been tried alone and without ſucceſs, it has probably ariſen from too great a quantity having been ſown. Be it raygraſs or rubbiſh, I underſtand, ſeldom leſs than a ſackfull an acre is thrown on: whereas ONE GALLON an acre, of CLEAN-WINNOWED REAL RAYGRASS-SEED, is abundantly ſufficient, on ſuch ſoil as the vale in general is covered with.

Or perhaps the miſcarriages have ariſen in the ſtrength of the vale lands ; in their being naturally affected by raygraſs, and in the want of theſe valuable qualities being duly tempered by proper management. (See YORK: ECON: vol. ii. p. 89.)

The

The *forcing* quality of the firſt ſpring of graſs ſeems to be, here, well underſtood. "No matter how ſhort the graſs at this time of the year, ſo the cattle can get hold of it;—they are ſure to thrive amain."

The reaſon is obvious: there is not, at that ſeaſon, a blade of any other graſs than ray graſs: no alloy to lower its value: it has then full ſcope; and, in this caſe, the Glocefter-vale graziers experience its uſe, as ſenſibly as the Norfolk farmers: theſe, however, are grateful; becauſe they know the effect proceeds from raygraſs: but thoſe, unaware of the gratitude they owe, ſtand foremoſt to revile its character.

In Norfolk, and on the Cotſwold hills, the lands are comparatively weak, and have perhaps long been uſed to ray graſs: the graziers, there, find no difficulty in keeping it down in the ſpring. Here, on the contrary, the land is rich, is peculiarly affected by raygraſs, has much of it lain, for ages, in a ſtate of aration, and is of courſe peculiarly prone to the graſſes. The graziers, it is highly probable, are not aware of the ſtock it will carry, for a few weeks in the ſpring; twice, perhaps three times, as much as their old graſs grounds.

Some men ſenſible of the miſchievouſneſs of foul "hayſeeds",—and believing in the diabolical influence of *raygraſs*, have laid down lands with WHITE CLOVER alone; or with a mixture of white clover and TREFOIL; without any bladegraſs whatever.

This is certainly preferable to fouling the turf with weeds; but it is returning one ſtep back to the obſolete cuſtom of letting land lay down in its own way. There is a certain loſs of nutritious herbage in the outſet;—and the weeds, already in the ſoil, will of courſe occupy, in ſome degree, the vacancies which would be better filled by blade graſſes.

That land may be leyed without blade graſſes is certainly true: I have long ago practiſed this method of leying. (See MINUTES OF AGRICULTURE, date 20. May 1775.) But it was before I had ſeen the extraordinary effects of raygraſs, when properly managed, in the eſtabliſhed practice of Norfolk, See NORF: ECON. vol. i. p. 303.)

It is equally true, that moſt excellent graſs land may be obtained, without ſowing any ſeed

ſeed whatever. (See YORK. ECON: vol. ii. p. 84.) The impropriety of the practice is, however, evident. And ſowing one claſs only appears to be, no more than a middle way between that and good management.

Who would not wiſh to ſee the herbage of his leys, the firſt year, reſemble the better herbage of his old graſslands, without their weeds?

It is evident, that the prevailing herbage of the beſt graſs grounds of this diſtrict is compoſed of raygraſs and white clover. In Spring and Autumn, the ſurface is in a manner wholly occupied by them. All that the art of leying wants, to make it perfect, is a SUMMER BLADE GRASS, to ſupply the place of the natural ſummer graſſes of the old ſward.

But if we are unable to reach perfection, there is no reaſon why we ſhould not approach it as nearly as we can. A nutritious bite, in ſpring and autumn, is certainly better than a want of it at theſe times. By ſowing a *ſmall quantity* of raygraſs, and keeping this *cloſely paſtured in the ſpring*,—the ſummer graſſes, natural to the given ſoil, have little more impediment to their riſing, than they would have, if no raygraſs were ſown.

If, inſtead of a *gallon* of *clean raygraſs*, a *jackful of rubbiſh* be ſown, or if even a gallon of clean raygraſs be ſown and the herbage be ſuffered to run away wild in the ſpring, and get poſſeſſion of the ſurface, its evil effects cannot be ſaid to be owing to the nature of the plant, but to a want of judgment in the growers of it. Under proper management, it can do no harm: it can *ſmother* nothing but the bones of the cattle that eat it;—nor *exhauſt* any thing, but the pockets of their purchaſers.

I have been induced to ſay more on this ſubject, and to expreſs my ideas in ſtronger language, as ſome of the leading men of this diſtrict are *afraid* to cultivate raygraſs; and one, more particularly, whoſe management is deſervedly looked up to, is an open enemy to it. All I have to ſay farther on the ſubject is, that, *I verily believe*, I have no undue affection for any particular ſpecies of graſs. My leading principle of conduct, throughout the irkſome undertaking I have engaged in, is to ſtand with all my ſtrength againſt FALSE-GROUNDED

PARTIALITIES:

PARTIALITIES: whether I perceive them in myſelf, or obſerve them in others.

The ſubject before us is of the firſt importance, in rural economics: converting worn-out arable lands to a ſtate of profitable ſward is one of the moſt important operations in huſbandry; and is, perhaps, of all the other operations in it, the leaſt underſtood. The diſtrict under ſurvey contains twenty thouſand acres of land, which ought to undergo this change, with all convenient ſpeed. And, whenever it take place, ten to fifteen thouſand pounds a year, for ſome years afterward, will depend on whether it be judiciouſly, or injudiciouſly conducted.

NATURAL

28.

NATURAL GRASSES.

THE OLD GRASSLANDS of this diſtrict fall moſtly within the ſpecies LOWLAND GRASS and MIDDLELAND GRASS. The UPLAND it contains is too inconſiderable to claim particular notice; conſiſting merely of the marginal ſlopes; and the ſides and contracted ſummits of the hillocks which are ſcattered on its area.

I. LOWLAND GRASS. This conſiſts moſtly of COMMON MOWING GROUNDS,—provincially "meadows" *: in part, of COMMON PASTURE GROUNDS,—provincially "hams" †. Some incloſed

* It is obſervable that the GLOCESTERSHIRE MEADOWS do not lie in long *ſwaths*, as thoſe of the YORKSHIRE INGS, but in ſquare *plots*, marked by boundary ſtones. The HAY is private property, but the AFTERGRASS is generally common to the townſhip; either without ſtint; or is ſtinted by the "yard lands" of the common fields.

† HAMS are moſtly ſtinted paſtures: one, near Gloceſter, is however an exception.

inclofed property likewife comes within this divifion of grafslands: which, it is obferva-ble, are uniformly found and fully fwarded; their levelled furface rifing in fome places twelve or fifteen feet above the level of dead water. No *fens*, or *watery marfhes*, mix in the lowlands of the vale of Glocefter.

By NATURAL SITUATION, however, thefe lands are fubject to be overflowed; either by the Severn, or by the rivulets which crofs the vale; and owe no doubt the prefent elevation and levelnefs of furface to the fediment of floods.

In the immediate neighbourhood of Glocef-ter, there are not lefs than a thoufand acres of this defcription of grafsland; moftly of a rich productive quality. The ISLF OF ALNEY (a holm, or river-ifland, formed by a divarica-tion of the Severn) confifts wholly of it. It is not, however, peculiar to the Severn; but accompanies, on a more contracted fcale, the Chelt and other brooks and rivulets, into the area of the vale.

The SOIL of thefe lowlands is invariably deep: and of the fame quality and contexture at different depths. That of the ifle of Alney, and

and the other meadows near Glocefter, is about fix feet deep; an uniform mafs of fomewhat redifh loam.

It is obfervable, however, that the quality of this loam varies in different fituations. At the upper point of the ifland it inclines to a coarfe fand; while toward the lower extremity, it is fine almoft as filt. It is alfo obfervable that the furface lies higher in that than in this fituation. But thefe circumftances are ftrictly agreeable to the general effects of floods: that is, of foul water in a current ftate.

Another obfervable circumftance relative to the foil of thefe meadows is, that it is uniformly CALCARIOUS, in the degree of about five grains to a hundred; except near the furface; *in the immediate fphere of vegetation*; in which it difcovers no figns of calcariofity! A circumftance that appears to me extremely interefting.

Near Glocefter, this bed of loam is ufed as BRICKEARTH: and, without any admixture, affords bricks of an excellent quality. A new county jail, on the Howardian principle of feparate cells, and on a very extenfive fcale, is now building with bricks made from this earth; one hundred grains of which, in the fituation,

tuation, from which the earth of theſe bricks is taken, affords, by analyſis, five grains of calcarious earth, twelve grains of ſand, and eighty three grains of ſilt.

Another obſervable circumſtance relative to this ſoil is, that it reſembles, in COLOUR, the waters of the Severn in the time of floods. The waters of rivers, in general, are, in the time of flood (during freſhes or land-floods as they are uſually called) of a light brown, or ſtone colour. But thoſe of the Severn, in their paſſage through this part of Glouceſter-ſhire, are moſtly a light red, or what is generally underſtood by a cinnamon colour; owing, moſt probably, to particles of the red ſoils, weſt of the Severn, being ſuſpended among thoſe waſhed from the vales of Gloceſter and Eveſham: the colour varying as the rain, which cauſed the ſwell, fell more or leſs, on the redland country.

The banks of the Avon and the Chelt are free from this redneſs; as are the riſing grounds on either ſide of the Severn meadows in this neighbourhood: facts which, to my mind, demonſtrate, that theſe meadows are a creation of the floods of the Severn, ſince the riſing rifing grounds received their prefent form: confequently, that the extenfive flat, which they now occupy, was heretofore (and, perhaps, not many centuries ago) a WASH; over which the tide flowed; in the manner in which it ftill flows, over a yet more extenfive tract of furface in the neighbourhood of Newnham. A tract of furface, which ftill remains in an unprofitable ftate; but which, may we not venture to fuggeft, might poffibly be re claimed.

The nature of the SUBSOIL, likewife favors the above pofition. Beneath the mafs of loam, which I have termed the foil, lies a ftratum of earth, of a fomewhat lighter colour, but evidently partaking of the nature of the foil, which refts upon it; beneath this, a yet lighter coloured filt, exactly refembling the mud, which is ftill brought up from the fea, or from banks formed in the lower parts of the Severn, and left in quantity by every tide, wherever it can find a lodgement: and beneath this bed of mud (mixed in fome places with a coarfer fandy earth) lies, in red and white ftrata, the *natural fubfoil of the country*,—the ORIGINAL SURFACE;—as left by nature, or the convulfions ſions of nature, which appear evidently to have thrown the earth's ſurface into its preſent form.

This original ſurface would be covered by the tides with ſilt from the ſea, long before the lands, lying above it, were brought into an ARABLE STATE; to furniſh the river-floods with materials to give much addition to the covering; and yet a longer time before ART aſſiſted (as in all human probability it has) in raiſing the ſurface to its preſent height*.

The

* By obſervations during a flood, while the general level was covered, a part near its center (the town ham, &c.) appeared ſome two feet above the water. This part, in much probability, was the original ISLE OF ALNEY: an ancient name, which the preſent holm bearing that appellation, was the leſs likely to obtain, as tradition relates that the minor diviſion of the Severn, which now winds by the kays of Glocеſter, was originally a cut, made for the conveniency of navigation: a circumſtance that is corroborated by the plan of an ancient fortification, which appears to have extended conſiderably beyond the preſent river; and whoſe foundation, probably, is now buried, among the accumulation of ſoil, ſome feet below the preſent ſurface.

Theſe obſervations, I acknowledge, are not eſſential to a regiſter of the preſent ſtate of rural affairs: nevertheleſs it is intereſting to obſerve the changes which the face of nature, and with it rural affairs, have undergone: not in this inſtance only; but in various others of a ſimilar nature, in every quarter of the iſland.

The HERBAGE, with which the floods, time, and other circumſtances have furniſhed theſe lowlands, varies with the manner in which they have been occupied.

The herbage of the "hams"—or commons is, (as has already been intimated) in the ſpring, and in autumn more particularly, one continuous mat of RAYGRASS and WHITE CLOVER, with a portion of the CRESTED DOGS-TAIL: the bladegraſſes being of a ſuperior quality; ſaccharine in the firſt degree: particularly thoſe of the commons that are fed with ſheep; which keeping down the weeds, the finer graſſes are in full poſſeſſion. But the ſuperior quality and productiveneſs of theſe paſture grounds are not matters of ſurprize:—for, beſides the annual tribute of the floods, they have had the whole of their own produce regularly returned to them: while the mowing grounds have been annually robbed of a principal part of their produce; without having, perhaps, in general, had any return whatever made.

The herbage of the "MEADOWS" appears in the following liſt; the individuals of which were collected in the Iſle of Alney, and other diviſions

divisions of the extensive flat, which has been more particularly noticed. They are arranged agreeably to their degrees of frequency in those meadows; or as nearly so as the intention of the arrangement requires.

LINNEAN.	ENGLISH.
Lolium perenne,	—raygrass.
Trifolium repens,	—creeping trefoil *(a)*.
Trifolium procumbens,	——procumbent trefoil *(b)*.
Hordeum murinum,	—common barleygrass.
Phleum nodosum,	—bulbous catstailgrass.
Cynosurus cristatus,	—crested dogstailgrass.
Carices,	—sedges.
Anthoxanthum odoratum,	—vernal.
Alopecurus pratensis,	—meadow foxtailgrass.
Festuca fluitans,	—floating fescue.
Festuca elatior,	—tall fescue.
Agrostis alba,	—creeping bentgrass.
Agrostis capillaris,	—fine bentgrass.
Alopecurus geniculatus,	—marsh foxtailgrass.
Holcus lanatus,	—meadow softgrass.

Bromus

(a) Creeping trefoil; or *white clover*.

(b) Procumbent trefoil; or *trefoil*.

Bromus mollis,—ſoft bromegraſs.
Bromus —ſmooth bromegraſs
Avena flaveſcens,—yellow oatgraſs.
Poa trivialis,—common poe.
Poa pratenſis,—meadow poe.
Poa annua,—dwarf poe.
Sanguiſorba officinalis,—meadow burnet.
Lathyrus pratenſis,—meadow vetchling.
Trifolium pratenſe,—meadow trefoil *(c)*
Lotus corniculatus,—birdsfoot trefoil.
Ranunculus repens,—creeping crowfoot*.
Chryſanthemum Leucanthemum,—— ox-eye daiſey.
Centaurea nigra,—common knobweed.
Achillea Millefolium,—common milfoil.
Rumex Acetoſa,—ſorrel.
Rumex criſpus,—curled dock.

Rumex

(c) Meadow trefoil,– or *red clover.*

* Ckeeping crowfoot;---- provincially "creeping crazey"——is here eſteemed as a valuable ſpecies of herbage, while the common and the bulbous ſpecies, of this genus of plants, are conſidered as extremely pernicious; eſpecially among hay. This is a diſtinction, which does the attention of the vale farmers great credit. The fact appears to be, on examination, that the two latter are extremely acrid, and probably have a cauſtic effect on the mouths of the cattle, which eat it: while the firſt is perfectly mild and agreeable to the palate. A circumſtance, that is not generally underſtood.

Rumex obtusifolius,—broadleaved dock.
Leontodon Taraxacum,--common dandelion†
Hypochæris radicata,—- longrooted hawk-weed
Galium verum,—yellow bedstraw.
Ranunculus Ficaria,—pilewort.
Bellis perennis,—common daisey.
Dactylis glomerata,—orchardgrass.
Briza media,—tremblingrass.
Aira cæspitosa,—hassock airgrass.
Avena elatior,—tall oatgrass.
Festuca duriuscula,—hard fescue.
Juncus articulatus,—jointed rush.
Scirpus cæspitosus?—fluted clubrush?
Peucedanum Silaus,—meadow saxifrage.
Oenanthe pimpinelloides?—meadow drop-wort?
Heracleum Sphondylium,—cowparsnep.
Carduus palustris,—marsh thistle.
Serratula arvensis,—common thistle.
Urtica dioica,—common nettle.
Vicia cracca,—bluetufted vetch.
Phalaris arundinacea,—reed canarygrass.

† The Glocestershire dairymen have also observed, that cows have an aversion to the "bitter grasses"—(the DANDELION and HAWKWEED tribes) but that sheep are particularly partial to them; eating even their "blows."

Cardamine patensis,—common ladysmock.
Senecio aquaticus,—marsh ragwort.
Spiræa Ulmaria,—meadowsweet.
Lychnis Flos-cuculi,—meadow campion.
Ranunculus acris,—common crowsoot.
Ranunculus bulbosus,—bulbous crowsoot.
Pastinaca sativa,—wild parsnep.
Achillea Ptarmica,—goosetongue.
Potentilla Anserina,—silverweed,
Potentilla reptans,—creeping cinquefoil.
Cerastium vulgatum,—common mousear.
Galium palustre,—marsh bedstraw.
Prunella vulgaris,—selfheal.
Ajuga reptans,—meadow bugle.
Myosotis scorpioides,—scorpion mousear.
Plantago media,—middle plantain.
Plantago lanceolata,—narrow plantain.
Rhinanthus Crista-galli,—yellow rattle.
Colchicum autumnale,—autumnal crocus.
Allium vineale,—crow garlic.
Tragopogon pratense,—goatsbeard.
Thalictrum flavum,—meadow rue.
Tanacetum vulgare,—common tansey *.

Cerastium

* TANSEY. A very common plant, in this district; particularly on the banks of the Severn.

Ceraſtium aquaticum,—marſh mouſear.
Galium Mollugo,—baſtard madder.
Antirrhinum Linaria,--common ſnapdragon.
Geranium pratenſe,—crowfoot craneſbill.
Valeriana dioica,—marſh velerian.
Orchis maculata,—ſpotted orchis.
Polygonum Perſicaria,—common perſicaria.
Lythrum Salicaria,—ſpiked willowherb.
Symphytum officinale,—common comfrey.
Ranunculus Flammula,—common ſpearwort.
Caltha paluſtris,—marſh marigold.
Mentha hirſuta,—velvet mint.
Siſymbrium ſylveſtre,—water rocket.
Siſymbrium amphibium,—water radiſh.
Sparganium erectum,—common burflag.
Poa aquatica,—water poe.

The PRODUCE of theſe meadows varies: near Gloceſter they are occaſionally manured, with aſhes and ſweepings of different kinds. The par produce, in a midling year, is, I underſtand, about a ton and a half an acre; not unfrequently two tons. The hay of a fine quality.

II. MIDDLELAND GRASS. The principal part of the graſslands of the diſtrict belongs to this claſs. The MEADOWS and HAMS, tho' extenſive, are not equal, in quantity of ſurface, to the "grounds:" of which ſome of the incloſed townſhips principally conſiſt; and which ought, indiſputably, to form the principal part of every townſhip within the diſtrict: the area of the lower vale is in a manner wholly occupied by this ſpecies of graſsland.

The SOIL is the ſame as that of the arable lands. Almoſt every acre of it having, heretofore, been under the plow: lying in ridge and furrow, like the lands of the common fields. In the pariſh of Churchdown, there are graſslands which lie in high ſharp ridges, with ſides nearly as ſteep as thoſe of a modern pitch-roof. In general, however, they appear to have been ſomewhat lowered, previous to their being laid down, or ſuffered to lie down, to graſs. Toward Gloceſter the lands in general are narrower, and ſome of them nearly flat.

On examining the ſoil of a ground, which is deſervedly eſteemed the beſt piece of land in the neighbourhood it lies in (Down Hatherley); and which, though a riſing ground, bears no veſtige of the plow;—I found it as follows:

follows:—The first six inches, a strong loam (a mixture of clay and sand) free from calcarious matter:—from six to nine inches, a dark brown clay, very weakly calcarious:—at twelve inches, a similar soil, but somewhat more strongly calcarious:—from fifteen to eighteen, a stronger bluish clay still more strongly calcarious: a soil, or rather a subsoil, which probably runs a considerable depth

The first six inches I found thickly interwoven with fibres; which lessened in number as the depth increased; but, even at eighteen inches, the subsoil appeared to be full of them. Hence appears the value of a rich subsoil to grassland. This piece has never been plowed; because, perhaps, it never required plowing; its sward never failed it; continuing in full vigour through successive generations. It is observable, however, that the ground under notice does not shoot early in the spring; but its sap once in motion its growth is uncommonly rapid.

The HERBAGE of the grounds varies much with the nature of the soil; or, perhaps, more accurately speaking, with the quality of the SUBSOIL. The colder clayey swells (some of which are ſhamefully neglected) naturally run to an almoſt worthleſs herbage: the *wood feſcue*, the *coltsfoot*, the *ſilverweed*, the *fleabane*, the *common ſcabious*, and the *ſedges*, are too frequently ſuffered to occupy their ſurfaces: while the boggy tumours, which riſe at the feet of the hills, and bulge out by the ſides of rivulets; and the ſwampy bottoms which the rivulets too frequently are obliged to ooze through;—are nurſeries of the whole paluſtrean tribe.

The herbage of the grounds, in general, is however, of a ſuperior quality. The PASTURES, in ſpring and autumn, are (as has been mentioned) covered with carpets thickly woven with a few of the fineſt graſſes. In ſummer, however, the MOWING GROUNDS diſplay a moſt ample variety. The individuals, which form it, are arranged in the following liſt, agreeably to their degrees of prevalency; or as nearly ſo as the intention of the arrangement requires.

LINNEAN. ENGLISH.

Lolium perenne,—raygraſs.
Trifolium repens,—creeping trefoil.
Cynoſurus criſtatus,—creſted dogstailgraſs.

Trifolium

Trifolium pratenſe,—meadow trefoil.
Poa trivialis,—common poe.
Trifolium procumbens,—procumbent trefoil.
Lathyrus pratenſis,—meadow vetchling.
Lotus corniculatus,—birdsfoot trefoil.
Bromus mollis,—ſoft bromegraſs.
Bromus ,—ſmooth bromegraſs.
Hordeum murinum,—common barleygraſs.
Phleum nodoſum,—bulbous catstailgraſs.
Avena elatior,—tall oatgraſs.
Anthoxanthum odoratum,—vernal.
Agroſtis alba,—creeping bentgraſs.
Agroſtis capillaris,—fine bentgraſs.
Poa annua,—dwarf poe.
Feſtuca ſylvatica,—wood feſcue *.
Ranunculus repens,—creeping crowfoot.
Ranunculus bulboſus,—bulbous crowfoot †
Ranunculus acris,—common crowfoot.
Achillea Millefolium,—common milfoil.

Centaurea

* WOOD FESCUE. Very common on the *cold ſwells*; and every where on *ant-hills*: an intereſting circumſtance.

† The BULBOUS CROWFOOT is ſingularly prevalent in this diſtrict. In the middle of May, ſome of the grounds near Glouceſter, were hid under its flowers. The *leaves* of this ſpecies are more acrid even than thoſe of the common ſort.

Centaurea nigra,—common knobweed.
Heracleum Sphodylium,—cowparſnep.
Paſtinaca ſativa,—wild parſnep.
Serratula arvenſis,—common thiſtle.
Rhinanthus Criſta-galli,—yellow rattle ‡
Euphraſia Odontites,—red eyebright.
Leontodon hispidum,—rough dandelion.
Leontodon Taraxacum,—common dandelion.
Hypochæris radicata,—longrooted hawkweed.
Galium verum,—yellow bedſtraw.
Potentilla reptans,—creeping cinquefoil.
Plantago media,—middle plantain.
Plantago lanceolata,—narrow plantain.
Ranunculus Ficaria,—pilewort.
Bellis perennis,—common daiſey.
Dactylis glomerata,—orchardgraſs.
Holcus lanatus,—meadow ſoftgraſs.
Briza media,—common tremblingraſs.
Alopecurus pratenſis,—meadow foxtailgraſs.
Avena flaveſcens,—yellow oatgraſs.
Poa pratenſis,—meadow poe.
Feſtuca elatior,—tall feſcue.
Aira cæſpetoſa,—haſſock airgraſs.

Alopecurus

‡ YELLOW RATTLE. For obſervations on this plant ſee forward.

Alopecurus geniculatus,—marſh foxtailgraſs.
Juncus articulatus,—jointed ruſh.
Chryſanthemun Leucanth:—oxeye daiſey.
Peucedanum Silaus,—meadow ſaxifrage.
Rumex criſpus,—curled dock.
Rumex Acetoſa,—ſorrel.
Rumex obtuſifolius,—broadleaved dock.
Carduus lanceolatus,—ſpear thiſtle.
Urtica dioica,—common nettle.
Ceraſtium vulgatum,—common mouſear.
Stellaria graminea,—meadow ſtarflower
Plantago major,—broad plantain.
Prunella vulgaris,—ſelf heal.
Primula veris,—cowſlip.
Viola hirta,—hairy violet.
Convolvulus arvenſis,—corn convolvulus.
Veronica Chamædrys,—germander ſpeedwel.
Veronica ſerpyllifolia,—thymeleaved ſpeedwel.
Juncus campeſtris,—graſs ruſh.
Feſtuca duriuſcula,—hard feſcue.
Avena pubeſcens,—rough oatgraſs.
Trifolium fragiferum,—ſtrawberry trefoil.
Vicia Cracca,—bluetufted vetch.
Orchis Morio,—fool's orchis.

Tragopogon

Tragopogon pratenſe.—goatsbeard.
Daucus Carota,—wild carrot.
Agrimonia Eupatoria,—agrimony.
Artemiſia vulgaris,—mugwort.
Chærophyllum ſylveſtre,—orchardweed.
Galium Mollugo,—baſtard madder.
Geranium pratenſe,—crowfoot craneſbill.
Geranium diſſectum,—jagged craneſbill.
Vicia ſativa,—meadow vetch.
Vicia ſepium,—buſh vetch.
Lathyrus Niſſolia,—graſsleaved vetchling.
Primula vulgaris,—primroſe.

The above conſtitute the herbage of the ſounder, better ſoils: the following are ſuffered to inhabit; and, in ſome inſtances, to occupy excluſively; the colder leſs fertile ſwells; or the bogs and ſwamps that are ſuffered to remain in more genial ſituations.

Feſtuca ſylvatica,—wood feſcue.
Ononis arvenſis ſpinoſa,—reſtharrow.
Tuſſilago Farfara,—coltsfoot.
Potentilla Anſerina,—ſilverweed.
Hieracium Piloſella,—mouſear hawkweed.
Carices,—ſedges.
Melica cærulea,—purple melic graſs.
Cineraria paluſtris,—marſh fleabane.

Scabioſa

Scabiosa Succisa,—meadow ſcabious.
Carduus paluſtris,—marſh thiſtle.
Spiræa Ulmaria,—meadowſweet.
Stachys paluſtris,—clownſallheal.
Juncus inflexus,—wire ruſh.
Juncus effuſus,—common ruſh.
Achillea Ptarmica,—gooſetongue
Ajuga reptans,—meadow bugle.
Orchis maculata,—ſpotted orchis.
Orchis latifolia,—marſh orchis.
Myoſotis ſcorpioides,—ſcorpion mouſear.
Mentha hirſuta,—velvet mint.
Polygonum Perſicaria,—common perſicaria.
Polygonum amphibium,—amphibious perſicaria.
Caltha paluſtris,—marſh marigold.
Veronica Beccabunga,—brooklime.
Siſymbrium Naſturtium,—water creſs.

The PRODUCE of theſe up grounds varies with the quality of their reſpective ſoils. An acre and a half to two acres, of the better grounds, are allowed as *paſturage* for a cow: there are grounds which will nearly carry a cow an acre. The produce of *hay* from one to two tons an acre.

The MANAGEMENT of GRASSLAND, as practiſed in this diſtrict, requires an outline of deſcription, ſimilar to that which was found requiſite, in deſcribing the ſame important branch of huſbandry, as practiſed in the vale of Pickering. See YORK: ECON: ii. 123.

The GENERAL MANAGEMENT comprizes

1. Draining	3. Dreſſing	5. Manuring
2. Clearing	4. Weeding	6. Watering

1. DRAINING. Many of the grounds are ſhamefully liable to ſurface-water. The ſubject of ſhores, ditches, and ſurface-drains, has been repeatedly touched on, in the courſe of this volume: it might here be reiterated. A vale without ſhores, ditches, and SURFACE-DRAINS, is a diſgrace to its owners and occupiers.

Beſides a deficiency of ſurface drains much UNDERDRAINING is wanted: eſpecially in the boggy tumours which have been noticed. The *flats* of cold blue clay, ſome few of which there are, would be found more difficult to be improved by underdraining: the cauſe of their infertility is probably owing more to the retentive nature of the ſoil and immediate ſubſoil, themſelves, than to internal waters riſing toward

toward the ſurface. *That* gives a general coldneſs, which is difficult to remove: but the effect of *theſe* is partial; being cauſed by collected or communicating waters, too ſmall in quantity, or lying too low, to force themſelves out at the ſurface, as *natural ſprings*; but are ready to eſcape from their confinement as ſoon as an *artificial vent* is made for them. *

The colder *ſwells* might probably be aſſiſted very much by throwing the lands acroſs the ſlopes. See YORK: ECON: vol. i. p. 324.

2. CLEARING. The graſslands of this diſtrict, conſidering their age, may in general be ſaid to be well kept: owing perhaps to their having, in general, been occaſionally mown for hay, or ſwept in a ſtate of paſturage. Buſhes and anthills are leſs common here than in many other graſsland diſtricts. Some grounds are in high preſervation: not a buſh or an ant hill left to disfigure their poliſhed ſurfaces. There are others, however, in the oppoſite extreme of neglect. Their ſurfaces hid, and in a manner occupied, by reſtharrow and the ant

* In the VALE OF EVESHAM, I am informed, much underdraining has been done, and with good ſucceſs.

anthill fefcue: a ftage of diftemper which nothing but the plow can cure.

Some of thefe lands, it has been faid, have been given up to tillage. The reft have a right to undergo the fame falutary operation. It is voluntary wafte, in their owners,—to let them lie in their prefent ftate; and that, too, without being repaid in any counter gratification. An oak-wood may be an object of *pride* to its owner; and grows venerable as it grows old: but a rough grafs-ground is an eye-fore; a fcab which disfigures the face of a country; and grows offenfive with age.

Their motive, however, for fuffering thefe grounds to remain under circumftances fo difgraceful, may be more pardonable than may appear at firft fight. It may proceed from the evident ill ufage of thofe which have been permitted to be broken up. But this only leffens, and does not wholly wipe away the *crime* of keeping them in an unproductive ftate. If they have not been properly laid down again to grafs, the *neglect* is their own. See YORK: ECON: vol. ii. p. 94.

3. DRESSING. Molehills and dung are here fpread with common hay-forks; ufed with the

the back downward; ſwinging them right and left: tolerable implements for the purpoſe. Sometimes a buſh-harrow is drawn over the ſurface of the mowing grounds; which are ſometimes rolled; eſpecially thoſe which have been foddered on, and trodden up by the cattle. No moulding hedge, nor any thing adequate to it, is here in uſe; though it would be obviouſly uſeful. The ſledge which is now in common uſe for carrying hedging thorns &c. might, with a little alteration, be made to anſwer both purpoſes. (See YORK: ECON: vol. i. p. 279.)

One particular in the practice of dreſſing meadows, here, is noticeable. If a mowing ground be fed late in the ſpring, ſo as to render it doubtful whether, if the dungbe ſpread, it would be waſhed down below the cut of the ſithe before mowing time, it is picked off the ground and carried to the dunghill.

4. WEEDING GRASSLANDS. With reſpect to the *eradication* of weeds, I have met with nothing praiſe-worthy in this diſtrict. Some of the meadows are ſhamefully overrun with *docks*; while the hams, being unappropriated, are too frequently occupied by *thiſtles*

which I have ſeen growing in beds of an acre each.

But with reſpect to the *topping* of weeds, in the incloſed paſture-grounds, the vale merits ſingular praiſe. It is the only diſtrict, in which I have obſerved this piece of good huſbandry, in any thing like common practice. Here, not only weeds of paſture-grounds are topped, generally once (about midſummer) and ſometimes twice; but the graſs of the furrows is mown, and the broken graſs of the ridges ſwept off for hay. Several loads of good fodder will ſometimes be got from a ground by this practice. A practice which ought to be adopted in every diſtrict. Beſides the loads of fodder which are obtained,—ſeveral acres of autumnal paſturage are probably gained:—or in other words a freſh ground is added to the farm—by the operation. See NORF: ECON: min. 7. and YORK: ECON: vol. ii. p. 150.

5. MANURING. The manuring of graſs-lands will, I believe, ſcarcely admit of being called a practice of *this* vale. The lowlands in general are conſigned to the benevolence of the floods: cowgrounds, which are every year paſtured, require no manure; and mowing grounds

grounds are ſeldom, I believe, afforded any. The arable lands, alone, require more than the diſtrict produces. However, by bottoming the courts with mould, to abſorb and retain that which now runs waſte out of them, a conſiderable quantity of graſsland manure might annually be obtained, without robbing the arable lands of a ſingle load of their preſent quantity of dung. See YORK: ECON: i. 405.

This deprivation of manure may account in ſome meaſure for the unproductiveneſs, compared with the intrinſic quality, of ſome of the vale lands; which may not, perhaps, have received any other melioration than the *teathe* of paſturing cattle, and perhaps ſome good effect from being foddered on in the winter, ſince the time they were converted into graſslands.

6. WATERING. The watering of graſslands, on the modern principle of float-and-drain, is not the practice of either of the vales of Glouceſterſhire. I have not ſeen even a ſingle inſtance in either of them; though there are many ſituations which would admit of its introduction. This circumſtance is the more remarkable, as in Northwiltſhire, a neighbouring diſtrict, it is in common practice. In

the more weſtern counties it is, I underſtand, ſtill more prevalent.

This is another inſtance of the ſtagnant ſtate of the huſbandry of theſe vales. It is highly probable, that, at the time of the diſſolution of the monaſteries, they ſtood pre-eminent in Engliſh Huſbandry. But, through an evident neglect of MODERN IMPROVEMENTS, they are now left, in many reſpects, beneath the reſt of the kingdom. This appears to me a circumſtance well entitled to the attention of the landed intereſt of theſe vales.

The OBJECTS of the graſsland management are *hay* and *paſturage.*

It ſeems to be well underſtood here, that grounds ought to be mown and paſtured alternately; and in ſome inſtances the principle may be attended to in practice. But it is generally convenient to have the "cow-grounds" near the milking yard. The diſtant grounds are of courſe more convenient as "mowing grounds:" they are, however, "grazed" occaſionally by fatting cattle.

It is obſerved here, and is obſervable almoſt every where, that if graſs land be mown every year it is liable to be overrun with the YEL-

LOW

LOW RATTLE (Rhinanthus) which, being a biennial plant that ſheds its ſeed early in the ſpring, is increaſed by mowing. But paſturing the ground, even one year, is found to check it. The reaſon is obvious: the major part of the plants, being eaten off with the other herbage, are prevented from ſeeding. Paſturing two years, ſucceſſively, and carefully ſweeping off the ſtale herbage, when this plant appears in full blow, would go near to extirpation.

The MANAGEMENT of

1. Mowing grounds,
2. Paſture grounds.

I. MOWING GROUNDS.

1. Spring management
2. Hay.
3. Aftergraſs.

1. SPRING MANAGEMENT of MOWING GROUNDS. In this diſtrict, where graſslands vary much as to their times of vegetating in the ſpring, the time of ſhutting up the *incloſed grounds* for hay, provincially "hain-"ing" them, is regulated by the nature of the land. Cold backward lands are ſeldom eaten in the ſpring: while the free-growing

more early grounds are paſtured till the beginning of May. This diſtinction is a maſterſtroke of management, which I have not obſerved in the ordinary practice of any other diſtrict.

The time of ſhutting up *meadows* is guided by cuſtom. Some Candlemas, others Lady-day, others May-day. A very extenſive meadow, immediately below the town of Glocester, is, by ANCIENT PRIVILEGE, paſtured, even with ſheep, until the middle of May. The conſequence of this cuſtom is, that in caſe the ſpring ſet in droughty, the crop of hay is in a manner loſt. This year (1788) the worm-caſts were not hid, until the latter end of June!

But injudicious as that RELICK OF ANCIENT LORDLINESS may now be, viewed in a general light, another, in its tendency abundantly more miſchevous, is preſerved in a meadow of ſome hundred acres, in the ſame neighbourhood. Over this valuable tract of mowing ground, two horſes range at large, *while the crop is growing!!!* with, of courſe, the privilege of doing all the miſchief to which the wantonneſs of horſes turned looſe in ſo

large

large a paſture can ſtimulate. The reader, I am afraid, will ſcarcely give me credit for what I am relating. No other authority than my own ſight could, I confeſs, have induced me to believe, that an evil ſo great—an abſurdity ſo glaring—could, in theſe enlightened and liberalized times, have exiſted in the rural economy of this country. Tradition ſays, that ſtallions, alone, were formerly entitled to this diabolical priviledge; but, at preſent, any two horſes are admitted to it. Whatever may have been its origin, it would be doing injuſtice to the preſent laws of England to ſuppoſe them capable of giving countenance to any act whoſe main tendency is the wanton deſtruction of the produce of the ſoil. No man has now a privilege of doing the community wanton miſchief. The full value of the paſturage is, no doubt, the rightful property of the *claimant*.

2. HAY. The ſtate of ripeneſs—*the age*—at which a crop of graſs ought to be cut—is a ſubject of no ſmall importance. In the ordinary practice of this diſtrict, as in that of every other diſtrict I have obſerved in, graſs is ſuffered to ſtand much too long, before it be

mown for hay. This evil practice may have originated in common meadows, whose after-grass is unstinted, (or frequently belongs to a separate owner): a species of mowing ground, which, formerly, was common to this and most other countries.

There are, however, in this district, men who are well aware of the advantages of early cutting;—who know, from experience in *grazing*, the value of the aftergrass of early mown grounds; as well as the fatting quality of hay, which has been mown in the fullness of sap. Hence we find in this country, more advocates for early cutting, than in most others, where the fatting of cattle on hay is not a practice. There is, in an ordinary season, much grass cut, in different parts of the district, *at six or seven weeks old.*

In *mowing*, it is observable, the Glocestershire labourers cut remarkably level. In some cases not a stroke, or scarcely a swath-balk, is discoverable. This is chiefly owing to the narrowness of the swath-width, and the shortness of the sithe, in use in this country. The mowers of Glocestershire and those of Yorkshire work in opposite extremes of the art.

The

The Yorkſhireman drives a width of nine or ten feet before him, the Glocesterſhireman of ſix or ſeven feet only. I have meaſured acroſs a ſeries of ſwaths which, one with another, have not meaſured ſix feet wide. The one makes the operation unneceſſarily laborious, and cauſes, almoſt unavoidably, a waſte of herbage,—the other renders it unneceſſarily tedious. A good workman may take *half a rod* (eight feet and a quarter) with ſufficient eaſe to himſelf, and at the ſame time leave his work ſufficiently level. It is prudent, however, on the part of his employer to ſee that he keeps within due bounds; and, generally, that he does not exceed the *medium width.*

The *making* of hay is an inexhauſtible ſubject. Every diſtrict, if we deſcend to minutiæ, has its ſhades of difference. The practice of this diſtrict reſembles very much the practices of Yorkſhire; not only in the firſt ſtages, but in the remarkable expedient of forming the hay into ſtacklets (here called "windcocks") previous to its being put into ſtack. But the practice is here carried a ſtage farther; the hay being ſometimes made into ſmall ſtacks, of ſeveral loads each, in the ſtack yard;

yard; and, while yet perhaps in a degree of heat almoſt ſuffocating to work among, is made over again into one large ſtack.

The ſame reaſons are given for this practice, here, as in Yorkſhire: namely that of being able to make it fuller of ſap in this way than it can be by the ordinary method. There ſeems, however, to be an additional motive to it in this country: namely that of being enabled, by this means, to make it into *very large ſtacks*—of fifty or perhaps a hundred loads each. Such ſtacks are faſhionable. They are ſpoken of with pride: and it ſeems probable that the *pride of great ricks* has ſome ſhare, at leaſt, in the practice of giving hay a double heat.

Be this as it may, however, it is a fact, well aſcertained, that the hay of theſe vales is of a ſuperior quality. It is found to bring on *fatting cattle* nearly as faſt as the green herbage from which it is made, paſſing thro' them with the ſame appearances. And the produce of *butter* from hay in this diſtrict, is extraordinary. But whether this ſuperior quality be owing, in part, to the method of making it, or wholly to the ſoil and the her-

bage

bage from which it is made, is by no means well aſcertained. That there is a *ſomething* in the ſoils of theſe vales, which gives a peculiar richneſs to whatever they produce, is to me evident; and to endeavour to preſerve in hay, as much as poſſible of this richneſs, is indiſputably, good management.

The *degree of heat*, which hay ought to be ſubjected to, is an intereſting ſubject, which is ſeldom agitated, and little underſtood; even in this country, where ſome little attention is paid to it. Something may depend on the ſpecies of ſtock it is intended for. The prevailing opinion, here, ſeems to be that, for fatting cattle, it ought to be moderately or ſomewhat conſiderably heated. For cows, however, there are dairymen, who ſay it ſhould have little or no heat; giving for a reaſon,—that "heated hay dries up their milk."—Theſe, however, I mention merely as opinions. They may be well grounded. If not, they may excite a ſpirit of enquiry into a ſubject of ſome importance in a graſsland country.

The *expenditure of hay* in this diſtrict is chiefly on cows and fatting cattle; to which it it is given either in ſheds—yards—foddering grounds—or the ground it grew on;—in the manner, which will be mentioned in the articles cows, and FATTING CATTLE.

3. AFTERGRASS. I find no regular management of it here. The unſtinted meadows are frequently turned into, the inſtant the hay is off the ground; and ſometimes while no inconſiderable ſhare of it remains in the meadow! Horſes, cows, ſheep, fatting-cattle, and haycocks being mixed in a manner ſufficiently *groteſque* for the purpoſe of the painter; but in a way rather diſguſting to thoſe, who are aware of the waſte they are committing: not of the hay, but of the aftergraſs. In eight and forty hours after the whole of the hay is out, the meadow, thus miſuſed, has the appearance of a ſheep common in winter: not a bite of green herbage to be ſeen; the whole being nibbled out by the ſheep and horſes, or trodden into the ground by cattle: nothing but the ſtubble, or dead ſtumps of ſeed ſtems, being left to cover the ſoil. Theſe meadows, however, being free of growth, ſheep, and even horſes, may continue to get a living on them; and cattle may be

be kept from ſtarving;—but cannot bring home any advantage to their owners*.

Nor is this illjudged practice confined within the unſtinted meadows; but is frequently extended to incloſed grounds. A full bite of aftergraſs is (this year at leaſt) a rare ſight in the country: I have ſeen very little fit for the reception either of cows or fatting cattle.

The line of right management is frequently difficult to draw. Different directions have their advantages and their inconveniences. By turning into mowing grounds as ſoon as the hay is out of them, the Gloceſterſhire farmer gives a looſe to his paſture grounds: it is a *move* for his cattle: and if he would forbear a few weeks, to let his aftergraſs riſe to a ſufficient bite, his management would, in my judgment, be much preferable to the Yorkſhire practice; in which the cattle are kept in the paſture grounds, without moving, until the aftergraſs be overgrown. See York: Econ. article aftergrass.

II. Pasture

* This, however, is not general. Some of them, by ancient cuſtom, are kept till the middle of September, before they be broken.

II. Pasture grounds.

1. Spring management.
2. Stocking.
3. Summer management.

1. Spring management. The hams and inclofed pafture grounds are fhut up at different times, and opened about Old May-day. Some of the hams much too late: thereby encumbering the furface, unneceffarily, with weeds and ftale grafs; and leffening, of courfe, the quantity of pafturable land*.

2. Stocking. It feems to be a prevailing cuftom to mix a few *fheep*, in the pafture grounds,——whether with *cows*, or *fatting cattle*.

3. Summer management. This appears in what has gone before. They are fwept, and fometimes mown; and have a refpite from ftock, while the *ftubbles* of the mowing grounds are picked over.

* See York: Econ: ii. 149.

HORSES.

29.

HORSES.

THE BREEDING OF HORSES for ſale is not, here, a practice. Moſt farmers rear their own plow-horſes; and a few ſaddle horſes are alſo bred: but I have met with nothing in the practice of breeding horſes, in this diſtrict, which requires to be regiſtered.

The farm horſes are of the fen breed:—but very uſeful ones of that ſort: ſhort and thick in the barrel; and low on their legs.—Colour moſtly black, inclinable to a tan-colour.

The price of a ſix-year old cart horſe, of this breed, is twenty five to thirty five pounds!

30.

SHEEP.

THE SHEEP is a MOUNTAIN animal. Even in its preſent cultivated ſtate, HILLS are its NATURAL ELEMENT. Uplands (or very ſound dry middlelands) are the loweſt ſtage on which ſheep can be *kept*, with any degree of ſafety to them; or with any degree of certainty to their owner. Vale lands, in general, are, without great caution, certain ruin to both.

Formerly, ſome conſiderable flocks were kept, or attempted to be kept, in this vale: even breeding flocks were not uncommon in it. But the wet ſummer of 1782, ſwept the country of them. One farmer, who had, for three or four years back, been recruiting his flock, and got it up to eight or nine ſcore, had not, I was informed, in the autumn of 1783, more than three individuals left!

The low ſituation of this vale,—the ſingular retentiveneſs of its ſubſtrata,—and the wa-terineſs

terineſs of its ſoils, through a want of ſurface-draining,—conſpire to render it,—what, from experience, it is too well known to be,—ſingularly fatal to ſheep.

How unaccountable, then, is the conduct of thoſe, who attempt to keep ſtore flocks in it? Nothing but the common error, which pervades almoſt every diſtrict,—that ſheep are eſſential to farming,—can account for it.

At preſent, however, the vale, fully convinced of the folly of attempting to keep ſtore flocks, changes its ſtock of ſheep every year.

This ſpecies of ſtock, now, conſiſts chiefly of ewes, bought in autumn, and, having fatted their lambs in the ſpring, are themſelves finiſhed in the courſe of the enſuing ſummer.

I. The SPECIES of ſheep uſed in this practice are moſtly the *Ryland*, and the *Cotſwold*; both of which will be deſcribed in the courſe of theſe volumes.

II. Some little FOLDING was formerly done in the fallow fields: "but all the folding flocks are dead of the rot"! What folly! What *cruelty*—to drive this animal from its native heights; and force it into a ſituation, where it muſt inevitably become a prey to diſeaſe;

eaſe; and at length, (if not releaſed by the humanity of a butcher), fall a victim to folly, by a loathſome, tedious, lingering death.

III. In a diſtrict ſo notorious as this for the ROTTING OF SHEEP, ſome accurate ideas of this fatal diſorder were of courſe enquired after. An experienced huſbandman, on opening a ſheep which he had killed for his own family, and finding a collection of water within it, pronounced the reſt of his flock to be tainted. Water he has always found to be the firſt ſtage of the diſorder: a "white ſcum" upon the liver the next: the laſt flukes. From theſe circumſtances, and from all the obſervations I have myſelf been hitherto able to make on this ſubject, it appears to me *probable*,—that *an unnatural redundancy of water* —unavoidably taken in with the food—is the cauſe of the diſorder.

CATTLE.

31.

CATTLE.

CATTLE are the natural inhabitants of a vale country; and in this vale we find every defcription of them abound:—COWS;—REARING STOCK;—FATTING CATTLE;—and each of thefe of various fpecies, or breeds.

Formerly, and perhaps not long ago, *one* breed of cattle might be faid to poffefs the vale; a breed which ftill predominates in fome parts of it. It is known by the name of the GLOCESTERSHIRE BREED; and has, I underftand, been common to the diftrict time immemorial. WELCH CATTLE, no doubt, may have long been brought into the diftrict, as *fatting cattle*; and of late years fome confiderable number of HEREFORDSHIRE OXEN have been fatted in it. But ftill the *cows* and *rearing cattle* were of the Glocefterfhire breed.

Of ftill later date, however, an alien breed of *cows* has been introduced: the long-horned breed of Staffordſhire and the other midland counties;--by the name of the "NORTH-COUNTRY SORT." A breed, that, in a few years, has made rapid advances; and is likely to diſpoſſeſs, in no great length of time, the naturalized ſpecies. In 1783, dairies were moſtly of the Glooceſterſhire breed: in ſome, a mixture of the longhorned ſort was obſervable;—and, in the lower vale, a few dairies were moſtly of that breed. Now (1788) few dairies are left without admixture; and, even in the upper vale, are ſome entire dairies of the longhorned breed. In general, however, they are an unſightly mixture of the two ſpecies; with, not unfrequently, a third ſort, a mongrel kind, reared from an aukward croſs between them. In the fairs and markets of the vale, ſcarcely any other than the north-country ſort and this mule breed are to be ſeen.

Of the LONGHORNED CATTLE of the midland counties I mean to ſpeak fully at a future time. WELCH CATTLE are extremely various: every province of the principality ſeems to ſend out a ſeparate breed. They are invariably of the middlehorned ſpecies; but in regard

gard to ſize they vary, in regular gradation, from the largeſt ox to the loweſt Welch runt. The HEREFORDSHIRE BREED will be ſpoken of under the head FATTING CATTLE; and in the article HEREFORDSHIRE, toward the cloſe of theſe volumes. The Gloceſterſhire, therefore, is the only breed which requires to be deſcribed in this place.

The GLOCESTERSHIRE BREED OF CATTLE is a variety of the MIDDLE HORNED SPECIES. (See YORK: ECON: article CATTLE.) In ſize, it forms a mean between the *Norfolk* and the *Herefordſhire* breeds. (See NORF: ECON: art: CATTLE.) The head moſtly ſmall; neck long; ſhoulder fine; and all of them generally clean. The carcaſe moſtly long, with the ribs full and the barrel large in proportion to the cheſt and hind-quarters. The huckle of due width; but the nache frequently narrow. The bone, in general fine; the hide thin and the hair ſhort. The characteriſtic colour, dark red,—provincially "brown";—with the face and neck inclining to black; and with an irregular line of white along the back. The horns fine and rather long; but, in ſome individuals, placed aukwardly high on the forehead, and near at the roots: in others, however, they ſtand low and wide; winding with a double bend, in the middle-horn manner.

The principal objections to the Glouceſterſhire breed of cattle are, a deficiency in the chine, and too great length of leg; giving the individuals of this deſcription, an aukward, uncouth appearance.

But no wonder. The breed has not had a fair chance of excelling. I have heard of only one man, within memory, who ever paid any eſpecial attention to it; and this one man, * by ſome election ſtrife (a curſe in every county) was driven out of the vale about ſeven years ago: ſo that, at preſent, it may be ſaid to lie in a ſtate of neglect. Nevertheleſs, it ſtill contains individuals which are unobjectionable;—particularly the remains of the BODDINGTON BREED; and, with a little attention, might, in my opinion, be rendered a very valuable breed of cattle.

For *dairy* cows, I have not, in my own judgement, ſeen a better form. It is argued, however,

* Mr. —— Long of Boddington.

however, that the northcountry cows, being *hardier*, ſtand the winter better in the ſtraw-yard; and *fat* more kindly when they are dried off. It ſhould be recollected, however, that Glocesterſhire is a *dairy* country: and remembered that it was the Glocesterſhire breed which raiſed the Glocesterſhire dairy to its greateſt height. Beſide, the breed has long been naturalized to the ſoil and ſituation;—and certainly ought not to be ſupplanted, without ſome evident advantage; ſome clear gain, in the outſet; nor even then, without mature deliberation; leaſt ſome unſeen diſadvantage ſhould bring cauſe of repentance in future.

The three claſſes, enumerated at the head of this article, now require to be ſeparately conſidered.

I. Cows. This being a dairy country, the *procuring* of cows, and the *ſize of dairies*; as well as the *treatment*, the *application*, and the *diſpoſal* of cows, will require to be ſhewn ſeparately.

1. PROCURING. Dairymen in general *rear* their own cows: ſome, however, *purchaſe* the whole, and others part, of their dairies.

The *point* of a milch cow which is here principally attended to,—and which, no doubt, is the main object of attention,— is a LARGE THIN-SKINNED BAG. I have, however, heard a large tail spoken of, in the true tone of superstition.

The following are the dimensions of a cow of the Boddington breed. A genuine, and a fair specimen, as to form; but not as to size: the cows of that celebrated breed were, in general, considerably larger. As a *milker* she has had few equals; and, in my eyes, she is, or rather was, one of the handsomest and most desireable *dairy* cows I have yet seen. These dimensions were taken when she was five years old, off; she being then several months gone with her fourth calf.

Height at the withers four feet three inches.

———--of the fore dug twenty one inches.

Smallest girt six feet and half an inch.

Greatest girt seven feet eleven inches.

Length from shoulder-knob to huckle four feet one inch.

———--from the huckle to the out of the nache twenty inches.

Width at the huckle twenty two inches.

Width

Width at the nache fourteen inches.

Length of the horn twelve inches.

The eye full and bright.

The ears remarkably large.

The head fine and chap clean.

The boſom deep; and the briſket broad, and projecting forward.

The ſhoulders thin with the points ſnug.

The thigh likewiſe thin, notwithſtanding the great width at the nache.

The bag large and hanging backward; being leathery and looſe to the bearing.

The teats of the middle ſize; gives much milk, *and holds it long*.

The tail large, the hide thin, and the bone remarkably fine.

The colour a "dark brown"; marked with white along the back and about the udder; with the legs, chap, and head, of a full, gloſſy, dark, chocolate colour.

The horns a poliſhed white; tipped with black.

The reaſons given, by the dairymen of this diſtrict, for *rearing* their own cows are, "that they ſhould ſoon be beggared if they had their cows to buy"; and "that they know what they breed,

breed, but do not know what they buy." The latter has much the moſt reaſon in it; for, as they obſerve, if a heifer is not likely to turn out well, they ſell her: on the contrary, if they went to market for their cows they muſt buy the outcaſts of other breeders. Beſides, they endeavour to breed from known good milkers; ſuch as milk well, not only preſently after calving; but will *hold their milk*, through the ſummer, and the lattermath months: whereas in the market they are ſubject to chance, and the deceptions of drovers: the moſt they have to judge from is the *ſize* of the bag at the time of the purchace. In ſuitable ſituations, there can be little doubt of the propriety of every dairyman's rearing his own cows.

The *place of purchaſe*, in this diſtrict, is chiefly the market of Gloceſter, held every Saturday; to which, in the ſpring, from fifty to a hundred cows, of different breeds, *with calves by their ſides*, are brought; by dairymen and drovers; but principally longhorned cows, brought from a diſtance by the latter. In the Ladyday fair at Gloceſter, there were not leſs than four hundred cows.

Some

Some of the larger dairymen go themſelves into the midland counties, to purchaſe cows. But ſeldom, perhaps, with much advantage; the expence of the journey; the time loſt; and the danger of a long drift, by unſkilful hands, probably, more than over-balance the dealer's profit. In caſes, in which ſtock is required to be transferred from one diſtrict to another, dealers become a uſeful claſs of men.

The *price* of a cow and calf of the Glocestershire breed, has been for the laſt ten years eight to ten or eleven pounds; of the north country ſort ten to twelve or thirteen pounds.

2. THE SIZE OF DAIRIES. In *this* vale dairies are not very large: twenty or thirty cows are a full ſized dairy. Forty, I believe, the higheſt*. But farms are ſmall, and of courſe numerous; and the number of cows kept are collectively very conſiderable.

3. TREATMENT OF COWS. Notwithſtanding, however, the number of cows which are kept in this diſtrict, and the length of time which it has been celebrated as a dairy country,

* In the VALE OF EVESHAM dairies are larger; fifty, ſixty, ſeventy, and one or two of eighty cows each.

try, I have met with few particulars in its management of cows, that are entitled to a place in this regifter.

The *fummer* management confifts chiefly in turning them out, in the beginning of May, fooner or later, according to the feafon and the nature of the foil,—into a ground, or fuite of grounds lying open to each other,—and there letting them remain until fome aftergrafs be ready to receive them. The *fhifting* of cows, from pafture to pafture, is fpoken of, and may be fometimes practifed by a few individuals; but it is not the general practice of the country.

The *winter* management varies with the characteriftic of the farm, as to grafs and arable. On farms which have much plowland belonging to them, the dry cows are kept in the ftraw yard, until near calving; when they are put to hay in a feparate yard, or a foddering ground. On farms which are principally "green," they are kept all winter at hay; in the open air, or under loofe fheds; the practice of houfing cattle in winter, in the north-of-England manner, being, it may be faid, unknown, in this quarter of the kingdom.

4. The

4. The APPLICATION of milk in this diſtrict, is to *calves*, *butter*, *cheeſe*; principally to the latter; which forms no inconſiderable part of the produce of a vale farm; and the DAIRY MANAGEMENT becomes, in this caſe, too important a ſubject to be confined, as heretofore, within a ſubdiviſion of the article CATTLE; requiring, in the preſent volumes, a ſeparate ſection. (ſee the next general head).

5. DISPOSAL OF COWS. *Dairy cows* are ſold, *with calves at their ſides*, in the manner which has been mentioned. *Heifers* which miſs the bull, or do not anſwer for the pail; alſo *young cows* that paſs their bulling; and *aged cows*, which are uſually thrown up at eight or nine years old, are, in the ordinary practice of the country, *fatted on the farm*, (in the way which will preſently be deſcribed) and ſold to the country butchers.

Thus, we find the dairymen of the vale of Gloceſter, not only rearing their cows from their own ſtock, but continuing them in their own grounds, after they have done their work as dairy cows, until they be fit for the ſlaughter:—-a ſyſtem of management, which is pleaſing

pleaſing to the obſervation; and which, by reaſon of its ſimplicity and perfection as a whole, affords the reflection equal pleaſure and ſatisfaction. There may be ſituations, which will not admit of this practice, in its full extent; but, in moſt caſes, there can be no doubt of its eligibility.

II. Rearing cattle. Breeding is here confined, in a manner wholly, to heifers for the dairy.

The number reared from a certain number of cows varies with circumſtances; ſometimes it may depend on the number of cow calves dropped within the ſeaſon of rearing; the demand for young cattle; the circumſtances of the farm; and the individual opinion of the dairyman,—likewiſe influence the proportional number. The firſt breeder in the vale, ſeldom reared more than ten or twelve calves from forty cows;—while another judicious dairyman reared nine or ten from twenty cows.

In giving a ſketch of the management of young cattle, in this diſtrict, it will be proper to ſeparate the three diſtinctions: namely,

Calves.
Yearlings.
Two-year-olds.

1. The

1. Calves. The *ſeaſon of weaning* laſts from Chriſtmas to Ladyday: ſeldom longer: late-weaned calves interfere with the dairy.

The *method of rearing* is pretty uniform: at leaſt in the outline. The calf is uſually taken from the cow at two or three days old, and put to *heated milk*. The degree of heat, however, varies. In the practice of the firſt breeder in the vale, the milk was given to the calves *ſcalding hot!* as hot as the dairy-girl could bear her hand in it. The lips of the calves were not unfrequently injured by it. His reaſons for this practice were, that the heat of the milk prevented the calves from ſcouring; made them thrive; and enabled him to put his rearing calves to ſkim milk, immediately from their being taken from the cow, at two or three days old. They never taſted "beſt milk" after they were taken from the teat at that age!

This is an intereſting inſtance of practice; and merits a few moments' reflection. Nature has evidently prepared milk of a peculiar quality for the infant calf; and this milk is uſeleſs in the dairy: it is therefore doubly good management to ſuffer the calf to remain

at

at the teat, until the milk becomes uſeful in the dairy; which it uſually does in two or three days. But although it becomes, to general appearance, ſimilar to that of a cow which has been longer in milk, it is highly probable, that it is *ſtill* ſingularly adapted to the yet infant ſtate of the calf. In the *ſuckling* houſes, round the metropolis, it is well underſtood, that putting a young calf to a cow, which is old in milk, will throw it into a ſcouring. It, no doubt, requires a degree of correction to render it fully acceptable to the ſtomach of the calf, at ſo early an age: and, if we may venture to judge from this inſtance of practice, *ſufficiently authenticated*, ſcalding the milk, very highly, gives it the due correction.

Beſides the ſcalded milk, this judicious manager allowed his calves ſplit beans, oats, and cut hay. When they took to eat theſe freely, water was, by degrees, added to the milk.

In the ſpring they were turned into a large well herbaged ground; allowing them ſo good a paſture, that it was generally mown after them: and, during the whole of the firſt

ſummer

ſummer, they had the firſt bite wherever they went.

"CALF-STAGES." The calf-pen of this diſtrict is of an admirable conſtruction: extremely ſimple; yet ſingularly well adapted to its intention. Young calves,—fatting calves more eſpecially—require to be kept narrowly confined: quietneſs is, in a degree, eſſential to their thriving. A looſe pen, or a long halter, gives freedom to their natural fears, and a looſe to their playfulneſs. Cleanlineſs, and a due degree of warmth, are likewiſe requiſite in the right management of calves.

A ſtage which holds ſeven, or occaſionally eight calves, is of the following deſcription.—The houſe or room-ſtead, in which it is placed, meaſures twelve feet by eight. Four feet of its width are occupied by the ſtage;—and one foot by a trough placed on its front; leaving three feet as a gangway; into the middle of which the door opens. The floor of the ſtage is formed of laths, about two inches ſquare, lying lengthway of the ſtage, and one inch aſunder. The front fence is of ſtaves, an inch and a half diameter, nine inches from middle to middle, and three feet high:

high: entered at the bottom into the front bearer of the floor; (from which croſs joiſts paſs into the back wall) and ſteadied at the top by a rail; which, as well as the bottom piece, is entered at each end into the end wall. The holes in the upper rail are wide enough to permit the ſtaves to be lifted up and taken out; to give admiſſion to the calves: one of which is faſtened to every ſecond ſtave; by means of two rings of iron joined by a ſwivel; one ring playing upon the ſtave, the other receiving a broad leathern collar, buckled round the neck of the calf. The trough is for barley-meal, chalk, &c. and to reſt the pails on. Two calves drink out of one pail; putting their heads through between the ſtaves. The height of the floor of the ſtage from the floor of the room is about one foot. It is thought to be wrong to hang it higher, leſt, by the wind drawing under it, the calves ſhould be too cold in ſevere weather: this, however, might be eaſily prevented by litter, or long ſtrawy dung thruſt beneath it.

It is obſervable, that theſe ſtages are fit only for calves, which are fed with the pail; not for calves which ſuck the cow.

Fatting

Fatting calves are here kept on the ſtages, until they be ſold: rearing calves until they be three weeks or a month old; or until they begin to pick a little hay; when they are removed to a rack, and allowed greater freedom.

2. YEARLINGS. The firſt winter they are uſually allowed the beſt hay on the farm: and the enſuing ſummer, ſuch a paſture as conveniency aſſigns them.——A diſtant rough ground, if ſuch a one belong to the farm, is generally their ſummer paſture.

3. TWO-YEAR-OLDS. The ſecond winter, heifers are generally kept at ſtraw; except they have had the bull the preceding ſummer; in which caſe they are wintered on hay. But the moſt prevalent practice is to keep them from the bull until the enſuing ſummer; *bringing them into milk, at three years old.*

III. FATTING CATTLE. The diſtrict under ſurvey, does not anſwer fully the deſcription of a GRAZING COUNTRY: the DAIRY forms its grand characteriſtic. Nevertheleſs, there are numbers of cattle annually fatted within it.

There are two diſtinct ſpecies of grazing carried on in this vale. The one natural to a dairy country: namely that of fatting barren and aged cows: a ſpecies of grazing, which is purſued by *dairymen* and *farmers* in general: the other is that which more particularly characterizes a grazing country: namely, the practice of purchaſing cattle for the immediate purpoſe of fatting: a ſpecies of grazing, which is here carried on by a few opulent individuals only. Some of them, however, purſue it on an extenſive ſcale; and in a manner, which entitles it to particular attention.

Theſe two ſpecies of grazing require to be examined ſeparately. They are not only proſecuted by two diſtinct orders of men; but the food—the cattle—the method of fatting—and the market of each is different. In one, the cattle are generally finiſhed in *yards* or foddering grounds, abroad, in the open air, on hay alone. In the other they are moſtly finiſhed in *ſtalls*, on hay and oil cake.

1. FATTING IN THE YARD. The *foods*, or fatting materials, in this caſe, are ſolely GRASS and HAY. Sometimes the cattle, in this mode of fatting, are freſhened with ſummer graſs, and finiſhed with lattermath; but, more frequently,

frequently, they are brought forward with graſs, and finiſhed with hay; which, of this country, if well got, is found to force them on nearly as faſt as graſs.

Beſides the CULLINGS of the DAIRY, a conſiderable number of WELCH CATTLE, of the ſmaller kinds, and generally cows or heifers; and ſome few HEREFORDSHIRE OXEN; are fatted in this way.

The principal *place of purchaſe* of the Welch cattle is Gloceſter market; to which, every Saturday, in the ſummer, the autumn, and the winter months, conſiderable numbers are brought.

The *ſummer management* of this claſs of fatting ſtock is no way extraordinary, nor particularly inſtructive. A diſtant ground is generally aſſigned them, for the double purpoſe of keeping them from the bull, and of giving the dairy cows the grounds which lie more conveniently to the yard.

The *winter management* is entitled to more attention. It commences in the field, while the cattle are yet at graſs; they being foddered, there, with hay, as ſoon as the graſs begins to ſhrink; or ſharp weather ſets in.

The graſs done, or the weather becoming ſevere,—they are either brought into a *ſmall dry graſs incloſure,* (near the homeſtall)—provincially a "foddering ground"—where they have their fill of hay, given them three times a day, in round rodden cribs*, which are rolled

* RODDEN CRIBS. Theſe are a kind of large baſket; made of the topwood of willow pollards. A utenſil common to this country and to Lincolnſhire; though ſituated on oppoſite ſides of the iſland: but they are alike graſsland countries, wherein cattle are fatted on hay. They are about ſix feet diameter. The height of the baſket-work is two feet and a half; of the ſtakes three feet and a half; their heads riſing about a foot above the rim of the baſket. The width between the ſtakes twelve to fourteen inches. The ſize, that of large hedge ſtakes. The ſize of the rods vary from that of a hedge ſtake, down to a well-ſized edder.

In making theſe hay baſkets,—the ſtakes are firſt driven, in a ring of the required ſize, firmly into the ground.——Some of the larger rods are then wound in at the bottom, in the baſket work manner. Upon theſe the ſmaller rods are wound; the middle part of the work requiring the leaſt ſtrength; reſerving the largeſt for the top. In the winding and due binding of thoſe, the principal part of the art of "withy cub making" reſts. Some makers warm theſe thick rods in burning ſtraw: others wind them cold; one man drawing them in with a rope; while another beats them at the ſtake with a wooden beetle, until they acquire a degree of ſuppleneſs. They are moſtly made by men, who go about the country; and who, by practice, make them

rolled upon the ridges of the lands, as the ground gets foul or poachy;—or in *yards*—provincially "courts"—in which the hay is given to them in mangers, formed by a rodded hedge, running parallel with the outſide fence; or in cribs—provincially "cubs"—of different ſorts and deſcriptions, placed in the area of the yard.

Out of theſe cribs and mangers the eattle not unfrequently feed to their knees in dirt; having perhaps an open ſhed to reſt under; or perhaps only a ſmall portion of the yard littered for that purpoſe: yet ſuch is the ſagacity and cleanlineſs of this ſpecies of animal, that when they are at liberty to make choice of their bed, they will, if poſſible, chooſe it warm and clean. I have ſeen half

Q 4 a dozen

them very completely; winding in the top-rods ſo firmly and ſo regularly, that it is difficult to know, which has been the laſt put in.

In uſe, the cattle lay their necks between the tops of the ſtakes. Each being thus kept in its place, the maſter cattle are, in a degree, prevented from running round, and driving away the underlings. The cloſeneſs of theſe cribs prevents a waſte of hay, either by the wind, or by the cattle.

On the whole, they are uſeful, ſimple, cheap; and, if well made, will laſt ſeveral years.

a dozen fine oxen, worth, at the time I repeatedly obſerved them, twenty to thirty pounds a piece, fatting on hay, actually to their knees in dung; with only a corner of the ſmall yard they were penned in, littered with ſtubble; and this corner ſo ſmall there appeared to be ſcarcely room for the ſix to lie down together: nevertheleſs, their coats were always clean; and, if one might judge from the condition they were in, and the appearance of health and good habit they wore, they were perfectly ſatisfied with their ſituation. A fact which appears to me extremely intereſting. The yard in this caſe was entirely open, (excepting ſome trees which overhung it) but was well ſheltered from the north and eaſt.

The *progreſs* of this claſs of fatting cattle depends much on the given ſize. The Welch ſort, if purchaſed early in ſummer, will generally get ſufficiently fat, with graſs alone; and ſome cows the ſame: but in general theſe are finiſhed with hay. If cows, which are put to lattermath, do not get fat on hay, by Mayday, they are ſometi nes ſold, as forward ſtock, to *graziers* of this or other diſtricts.

tricts. The oxen are not expected to be finished completely in less than ten or twelve months.

The *purchasers* of this class (the oxen generally excepted) are the butchers of the district.

In estimating the value of fat cattle, here, the *butcher's allowance* of profit, on a cow of ten or twelve pounds price, is from one to two guineas.

The *proof* expected from this class of cattle, at head keep, is—Welch cows 1s. 6d. to 2s. dairy cows 2s. to 3s. oxen 3s. to 3s. 6d. a week, at grass; and somewhat considerably more at hay.

2. STALL FATTING. This may be considered as a modern practice, in the RURAL ECONOMY OF ENGLAND.

GRASS is the NATURAL food of fatting cattle. HAY was probably first in use for WINTER fatting. CORN has probably been used, on a small scale, time immemorial, for the same purpose. TURNEPS may have been applied to this purpose, in Norfolk, about a century. But OILCAKES, the residuum or bran of linseed from which oil has been expressed, (the

(the grand material made uſe of in the practice under notice) has not perhaps been uſed, in this intention, more than half that period. They have not in this diſtrict been uſed, in quantity, more than 20 to 30 years.

At preſent they are become a ſtaple article of food, for winter fatting, in various parts of the iſland; but in no one of the five widely diſtant ſtations, I have obſerved in, are they uſed on ſo ample a ſcale as in the diſtrict now under ſurvey. There are two individuals finiſh, annually, from one hundred to one hundred and fifty head of large bullocks each. And a third, who fats a ſtill greater number: not however on oilcakes, alone; but on the foods, and in the manner, which will be mentioned.

In giving a detail of this practice, it will be proper to take a ſeparate view of

1. The ſituation and ſoil of the diſtrict.
2. The foods or materials of fatting.
3. The breed, ſex, and age, of the cattle fatted.
4. The places of purchaſe and the obſervable points.
5. The ſummer management.

6. The

6. The winter management.
7. The market.
8. The produce.

1. *Situation.* This ſpecies of "grazing" is confined chiefly to the vicinities of Glocefter, Tewkeſbury, and Upton. The *ſoil*, whether of upland or meadow, is moſtly rich, ſound, and early. The upgrounds affording paſturage, and the meadows hay, of the firſt quality. If we except the margins of ſalt marſhes, few ſituations are better adapted to ſummer grazing; and the navigation of the Severn is favourable to winter fatting.—We may add to theſe advantages, the circumſtances of one of the fineſt breeds of cattle, the iſland affords, being reared on one hand; while the market of the metropolis is within a moderate diſtance on the other.

2. The *foods* in uſe for ſtall fatting are HAY, CORN, "CAKES", LINSEED.

Hay is a ſtanding article of food in the ſtalls; being uſed jointly with one or more of the other articles; moſtly, I believe, in its natural ſtate; ſeldom, I underſtand, cut with ſtraw into what is termed chaff; a practice in ſome other diſtricts.

The

The ſpecies of *corn* in uſe are barley and beans, ground, and given dry, alone. But this is not a common material of fatting in the diſtrict under notice, where

Oilcake, as has been ſaid, is, next to hay, the main article of ſtall fatting. But the price of this article is at leng thbecome ſo exorbitant, that it no longer, I am afraid, leaves an adequate profit to the conſumer. Some years back, I recollect, it was the idea of men of experience, that it could not be uſed profitably as an article of fatting for cattle, at a higher price than three pounds a ton. Now (1788) it is, in ſome places, more than twice that price. The loweſt price, at the more diſtant mills, is, I am well informed, five pounds; at Berkeley mills, ſix pounds; at Eveſham, ſix guineas; at Stratford, ſix pounds ten ſhillings a ton. †

This extravagant price of the cakes has induced ſome ſpirited individuals to try the *linſeed*, itſelf, boiled to a jelly, and mixed with flour,

†. Theſe prices fluctuating, from time to time, ſo much as 20s. a ton. Some few years ago the price was higher than it is at preſent.

flour, bran or chaff; and, from the information I have had, with favorable ſucceſs. *

This novel practice requires a few minutes reflection. From the preſent ſcarcity and dearneſs of cakes, it may be inferred that the demand is greater than the quantity in the markets. If, therefore, the ſeed can be profitably uſed; though with only a ſmall increaſe of profit, and with this even on a contracted ſcale; the uſe of it may operate very beneficially; by leſſening the demand, and thereby lowering the preſent exorbitant price, of the cakes.

It is highly probable, however, that it may be uſed with much greater advantage than cakes at their preſent price. I have by me a ſample of American ſeed, (nearly equal to the beſt Dutch ſeed I have ſeen), which may now be imported for 38 to 40s. a quarter, of eight wincheſter buſhels. Suppoſing the buſhel to weigh 50lb, the price of this prime ſeed is not twelve pounds a ton. Ordinary ſeed might be had cheaper.

It is farther *probable* that the ſuperior kind of nutriment, which the cakes afford, proceeds from

* In Herefordſhire, *linſeed oil*, I am told, is uſed in a ſimilar manner.

from the unexpreſſed oil they contain, rather than from the huſks of the ſeed of which they appear to conſiſt. This being admitted, and ſeeing the exceſſive power which is uſed in extracting the oil, we may without riſque conclude that a ton of ſeed contains more than twice (*perhaps* five times) the nouriſhment which remains in a ton of cakes. *

Viewing the preſent ſubject in a partial light, it might be ſaid, that an unlimited and exceſ-ſive

* LINSEED-JELLY. The principal objection to this material is the trouble of preparing it. In an inſtance in which it was uſed with ſucceſs, the method of preparing was this. The proportion of water to ſeed was about ſeven to one. Having been ſteeped, in part of the water, eight and forty hours, previous to the boiling, the remainder was added, cold ;—and the whole boiled, gently, about two hours ; keeping it in motion during the operation, to prevent its burning to the boiler ; thus reducing the whole to a jelly-like, or rather a gluey or ropy conſiſtence. Cooled in tubs: given, in this inſtance, with a mixture of barley meal, bran, and cut chaff ; each bullock being allowed about two quarts of the jelly a day ; or ſomewhat more than one quart of ſeed in four days: that is, in this caſe, about one ſixteenth of the medium allowance of cake.

This however is thrown out as a general idea ; not drawn as an Inference: the comparative effect of theſe two materials of fatting forms an important ſubject for the deciſion of experiment.

ſive uſe of a foreign article of fatting for cattle, might leſſen the demand, and thereby lower the value of our own productions, applicable to the ſame purpoſe; to the injury of the landed intereſt. If, however, we conſider that, by the uſe of foreign linſeed, an influx of the firſt vegetable manure we are acquainted with would be diffuſed over the ſoils of this country; and that wheat may be exported at a price more than equivalent to the preſent price of linſeed; the landed intereſt would ſeem to have no cauſe of alarm;—while in a more general point of view, the importation of linſeed from AMERICA might be a national good. I underſtand from intelligence of the firſt authority, that ſome of the fineſt provinces of that diſtreſsful country, are in a manner deſtitute of marketable returns, for the produce and manufactures of this kingdom; and further, that linſeed, which can there be grown in unlimited quantities, is at preſent a drug in the American markets.

But this by the way, FLAX SEED cannot yet be conſidered as an eſtabliſhed article of food for cattle, in this diſtrict; in which GRASS, HAY, and OILCAKE are the prevailing foods of of the ſpecies of fatting cattle now under conſideration ; and to thoſe, only, I ſhall confine myſelf in the following remarks.

3. *The cattle* which are ſubjected to this mode of fatting are chiefly HEREFORDSHIRE OXEN, which have been worked in the breeding country, and thrown up after barley ſeed-time, in working condition ; or have been kept over the ſummer, and ſold " freſh"—that is forward in fleſh—to the graziers in autumn.

Beſides theſe, ſome of the larger breed of oxen of South-Wales particularly of Glamorganſhire; alſo of Wyeſide of Gloceſterſhire, as well as round the foreſt of Dean, and in the over-Severn diſtrict ; alſo ſome Somerſetſhire, and ſome few Devonſhire oxen are fatted here ; but theſe, collectively, are few in proportion to thoſe of the Herefordſhire breed ; which, alone, I ſhall conſider as the objects of ſtall-fatting, in this diſtrict.

The AGE at which theſe oxen are uſually fatted is *ſix years old !*

I do not mean to cenſure the workers of theſe oxen, for throwing them up in their prime as beaſts of draught ; much leſs to blame the graziers for fatting them, or the butchers

butchers for ſlaughtering them in that uſeful ſtage of life; but I cannot help expreſſing my regret, on ſeeing animals ſo ſingularly well adapted to the cultivation of the lands of theſe kingdoms, as are the principal part of the ſix-year-old oxen of Herefordſhire, proſcribed and cut off in the fulneſs of their ſtrength and uſefulneſs.

The graziers, indeed, conſidered merely as ſuch, do not, in this caſe, come within the reach of cenſure. They know from experience that the cattle under obſervation genenerally leave them the moſt profit at that age. Some few individuals, however, will, it is ſaid, *grow* (that is, ſpread out in carcaſe) *as well as fat* (the two things deſireable to the grazier) at ſeven years old. But after thoſe ages, having ceaſed to *grow*, they pay for *fatting* only *.

It is, however, allowed that a full-aged ox *tallows* better than a young growing ox. But,

* I have met with an idea, in this diſtrict, that a gummy, thick-thighed, hard-fleſhed ox ſhould not only be kept to a greater age than one of the oppoſite deſcription; but ſhould be worked down low in fleſh, previous to his being finally thrown up for fatting.

But, on the other hand, it is argued that oxen which are hardly worked and hardly kept, become flat-fided, lofe the laxity of their fibres, and do not, on being fatted, fill up fo well in their points, as younger oxen, which have been lefs hardly ufed.

This, however, is not good argument againft the general pofition: oxen, whether young or old, fhould never be worked down into a ftate of poverty of carcafe: but ought, at all times, to be kept as full of flefh as their activity will permit. If horfes pay for being kept up in carcafe, while they are worked, how much more amply would oxen pay for a fimilar treatment.

But argument becomes fuperfluous where facts are produceable. There is one inftance mentioned in this diftrict, in which an ox was worked until he was FIFTEEN YEARS OLD, and then fatted "tolerably well".—And a ftill more valuable incident than this occurred in the practice of the firft grazier within the diftrict immediately under obfervation *; in which inftance *three* oxen were *finifhed* in the ufual time allowed for fix-year-old oxen; which

* Mr. DARKE of Bredon.

which three oxen were EIGHTEEN YEARS OLD; a fact that I have fingular fatisfaction in regiftering. †

4. *Purchafe* and *points*. The *places of purchafe* are the fairs of Herefordfhire: held at the different towns of the county, in almoft every month of the year; and thofe who purfue this fpecies of grazing, on a large fcale, may be faid to purchafe the year round. But fpring and autumn, as has been intimated, are the principal *times of purchafe*. Lean in the fpring, for fummer grazing; and forward, in autumn, for more immediate ftall fatting.

The *favorite points*, by which graziers make choice of the individuals of this breed of cattle, are *fimilar* to thofe which are obferved in other diftricts; yet they are not altogether the *fame*. In different diftricts I find graziers, in their choice of cattle, not only particularly obfervant of different points; but have, in fome meafure, diftinct criterions to judge by: and I am of opinion that different breeds or varieties of cattle require fuch a difference of judgement.

† Thefe oxen were bred and kept to that age, by Mr. Cook of the Moor, near Hereford.

Every variety of cattle has a tendency to degenerate; and each appears to have its peculiar propenſity in degenerating. Thus the Glocesterſhire breed become, under neglect, narrow in the cheſt, light in the hind quarters, and long upon the legs. The Herefordſhire breed,—get a lumpiſhneſs of carcaſe and a heavineſs of the limbs. The long-horned breed, on the contrary become gaunt in the carcaſe, coarſe in the forehand, and thick in the hide. While the Holderneſs breed tend to a gummineſs of the hind-quarters and a hardneſs of fleſh.

Theſe obſervations, however, are, at preſent, offered incidentally; to endeavour to reconcile the jarring opinions of profeſſional men on this ſubject. I perceive a captiouſneſs, in every diſtrict, among men who ſtand high in their profeſſion; ariſing from a partiality toward the particular breed they are moſt converſant with; and from a want of a more general knowledge of the ſeveral breeds of the iſland at large.

The profits of grazing reſt, in a great meaſure, on the proper choice of the individuals to be fatted; be the ſpecies or the variety what

what it may. And although a quick and accurate judgement, in this caſe, as in almoſt every other, can be matured by practice, only; yet the groundwork is certainly reduceable to ſcience. If from men of experience, and ſuperior judgement, we can aſcertain the criterions of good and bad qualities of the ſeveral breeds of the animals to be fatted, the ſtudent will be enabled to acquire the requiſite judgement much *ſooner* than he could without ſuch aſſiſtance.

From my own obſervations, corrected and made more full and perfect by thoſe whoſe experience has rendered them adequate judges of the ſubject, I am fully authorized, I truſt, to ſet down the following as deſireable qualities in the Herefordſhire breed of oxen.

QUALITIES *deſireable* in a Herefordſhire ox, intended for GRAZING.

The *general appearance* full of health and vigour; and wearing the marks of ſufficient maturity;—provincially "oxey"—not "ſteeriſh"—or ſtill in too *growing* a ſtate to *fat*:

The *countenance* pleaſant; chearful; open; the forehead broad:

The *eye* full and lively:

The *horns* bright, taper, and fpreading:

The *head* fmall, and the chap clean:

The *neck* long and tapering:

The *cheft* deep; the bofom broad *, and projecting forward. †

The *fhoulder-bone* thin, flat; no way protuberant, in bone; but full and mellow, in flefh.

The *chine* full.

The *loin* broad.

The *hips* ftanding wide; and level with the fpine.

The *quarters* long; and wide at the nache.

The *rump* even with the general level of the back: not drooping; nor ftanding high and fharp above the quarters. The *tail* flender, and neatly haired.

The *barrel* round, and roomy: the carcafe throughout being deep and well fpread.

The *ribs* broad; ftanding clofe; and flat on the outer furface; forming a fmooth even barrel: the hindmoft large, and of full length.

The *round-bone* fmall; fnug; not prominent.

The

* In a WORKING OX this is a moft defireable point.

† This is, here, a very popular point, whether in a cow or an ox.

The *thigh* clean, and regularly tapering.

The *legs* upright and ſhort. *

The *bone*, below the knee and hough, ſmall. †

The *feet* of a middle ſize.

The *cod* and twiſt round and full.

The *flank* large.

The *fleſh* every where mellow; ſoft; yielding pleaſantly to the touch; eſpecially on the chine, the ſhoulder, and the ribs.

The *hide* mellow; ſupple; of a middle thickneſs; and looſe on the nache and huckle.

The *coat* neatly haired, bright, and ſilky; its colour a middle red—with a "bald face": the laſt being eſteemed characteriſtic of the true Herefordſhire breed.

QUALITIES

* It may be diſputable whether the legs of a WORKING OX ought to be ſhort or of a middle length. Cattle are naturally heavier, leſs active, than horſes; whoſe legs are ſeldom found too ſhort in harneſs. Nevertheleſs, oxen may require ſome length of leg, to aſſiſt them in travelling. It is obſervable, however, that the beſt working ox, I have known, had remarkably *ſhort* legs.

† In a WORKING OX, the *ſinew* ſhould, nevertheleſs, be large.

QUALITIES *exceptionable* in a Herefordſhire ox, for grazing.

The *general appearance* ſluggiſh; ſpiritleſs; lumpiſh;—or aukward, through a deformity in make, or a want of ſufficient maturity.

The *countenance* heavy, ſullen,—"cloudy."

The *eye* hollow and dull.

The *horns* coarſe and thick; provincially "goary."

The *head* large, thick; the chap coarſe and leathery.

The *neck* ſhort, thick, coarſe; loaded with leather and dewlap; "throaty."

The *ſhoulder-points*—provincially the "elbows"—ſtanding wide;—or projecting forward *.

The *chine*—"keen";—that is, riſing ſharp above the withers;—and hollow behind the ſhoulders.

The *loin* contracted; narrowing to a point at the chine.

The *hips* ſtanding narrow; or placed below the general level.

The

* This is, here, ſpoken of as the moſt hateful point an ox can poſſeſs: while, in other diſtricts, it paſſes, comparatively, unnoticed. In a WORKING OX, it is, eſpecially in harneſs, a very great fault.

The *rump* drooping;—" gooſerumped;"—or the tail ſet on too high; ſtanding above the level of the ſpine.

The *quarters* ſhort, falling, and narrow at the nache.

The *barrel* contracted upward; the ribs dropping flat from the chine—" flatſided;"—forcing the intrails downward—" cowbellied."

The *ribs* narrow, and placed at a diſtance from each other; leaving vacancies between them; throwing the ſurface of the barrel into ridge and furrow.

The *round-bones* large; bulging out wide in proportion to the hips.

The *haunches* fleſhy;—" brawny."

The *limbs* in general large and unwieldy.

The *hind-legs* crooked inward at the gambrels; or the fore legs at the knees*.

The *ſhank* long and thick.

The *feet large*, with the claws ſpreading.

The *cod* flaccid; with the point hard and knobby.

The *flank* thin, ſingle.

The

* This is a defect, amounting, in ſome caſes, to an infirmity. I have obſerved it, in an inferior degree, in other breeds; eſpecially in the fore legs. In a WORKING OX, it is an inſurmountable objection.

The *fleſh*, on the chine and ribs, hard.

The *hide* harſh, thick, and ſticking to the carcaſe.

The *coat* ſtaring, — " ſett,"— not lying cloſe; appearing dead; faded; not alive and glowing:— ſymptoms, theſe, of a diſeaſed habit.

5. *Summer management.* The management of grazing, in this diſtrict, has been repreſented, aforegoing, as not being ſufficiently intereſting to require to be *detailed:* nor do I, in this department of it, find any *particulars* entitled to eſpecial notice. In ſaying this, however, I do not mean to intimate, that it is more reprehenſible, than that of other grazing diſtricts. Indeed it is not, in this caſe, the main object of practice; being only uſed as a preparation to STALL FATTING.

6. *Winter management.* This, for reaſons already given above, will require to be analyzed; and each part to be deſcribed in detail. And previous to this detail, it will be requiſite to deſcribe the building in uſe, here, for winter-fatting.

"OX-STALLS." What characterizes the bullock ſheds of this diſtrict, and diſtinguiſhes them

them from thoſe of every other, I have obſerved in, is the circumſtance of each bullock having a *houſe* and a *yard* to himſelf; in which he goes looſe; occupying them by turns, as appetite or amuſement directs him; having a manger and a drinking trough to go to at pleaſure. He, of courſe, eats when he is hungry, and drinks when he is thirſty. He is alſo at liberty to rub, or to lick himſelf; as well as to keep his body in a degree of temperature, as to heat and cold. Theory could not readily ſuggeſt more rational principles.

The conſtruction of theſe ſtalls varies in the minutiæ. The water trough, for inſtance, is ſometimes placed by the manger, in the hovel or ſhed:—ſometimes in the open pen. Other leſs noticeable variations may be ſeen in different buildings.

The plan and dimenſions, which, at preſent, ſeem to ſtand higheſt in eſteem; and on which ſeveral erections of this nature have been made within the laſt fifteen or twenty years; are the following.

The building fifteen to fifteen feet and a half wide within, and of a length proportioned

to

to the number of ſtalls required. The height of the plates ſix feet to ſix feet four inches; ſupported on the ſide to the north or eaſt by cloſe walling; on that to the ſouth or weſt by poſts, ſet on ſtone pedeſtals. The gables walling. The covering plain tiles, on a ſingle pitch-roof.

Againſt the back wall is a gangway, three and a half to four feet wide, formed by a length of mangers, three feet to three and a half feet wide, from out to out, at the top; narrowing to about fifteen inches within, at the bottom. The perpendicular depth fourteen or fifteen inches; the height of the top rail from the ground, about two feet nine inches. The materials two-inch plank; ſtayed and ſupported by poſts and croſs pieces; and ſtiffened by ſtrong top-rails.

The dimenſions of the area of the covered ſtalls, about eight feet three inches ſquare; of the open pens, the ſame.

The partitions between the ſtalls are of broad rails, paſſing from the outer pillars to ſimilar poſts, riſing on the inner or ſtall ſide of the manger; and ſteadied at the top by ſlender beams, reaching acroſs the building; each

each ſtall, or each partition, having a beam and a pair of principals.

The partitions of the pens are gates, reaching from the pillars to the boundary wall; and likewiſe from pillar to pillar. When they are fixed in *that* ſituation, each bullock has his ſtall and his little yard. When in *this* each is ſhut up in his ſtall; the yards forming a lane, or driftway, for taking in, or turning out, any individual.

The boundary wall of the pens is about four feet high; coped with blocks of copper-droſs. On the outer ſide of it is a receptacle for manure. On the inner a range of water troughs; with a channel of communication for the conveniency of filling them. The materials of the troughs, ſtone*; of the channel, gutter bricks, covered with ſlabs.

The

* STONE TROUGHS. Theſe troughs, which are about fourteen inches by two feet ſix inches within,—have a conveniency in their conſtruction, which is entitled to notice. Inſtead of the ſides and the ends being all of them pecked down to an angle, ſquare with the bottom, one of the ends is left bevelling, ſloping, making a very obtuſe angle with the bottom. This ſimple variation renders them eaſy to be cleaned; either with the ſhovel, or the broom.

The floor is paved with hard-burnt bricks, laid edge-way in mortar; being formed with a steep descent from the wall to a channel, some three or four feet from it; and with a gentle fall from the manger to the same channel; which becomes the general drain for rain water and urine.

At one end of the pens is a pump (where a natural rill cannot be had) for supplying the troughs with water; and, at the other, a stack of stubble for litter; which is used in the stall only; the yard being left unlittered.

At one end of the building is a cake-house, at the other, the rickyard; with a door at each end of the gangway to receive the hay and the cake.

In one or more instances, I have seen a double range of stalls on this plan; the area between them being the common receptacle for the dung. When a number of stalls, as twenty or thirty, are required, this arrangement brings them within a convenient compass; and the two ranges, with a proper aspect, become shelter to each other.

Beside these *loose* stalls, there are others, built nearly on the same plan, but without gates,

gates, and on a ſomewhat ſmaller ſcale, in which the cattle are *faſtened* to the manger, or the partition poſts, with a long chain, which gives them liberty to rub and lick themſelves, and move about in their ſtalls. In this caſe, a water trough is generally placed at the end of every ſecond partition, level with the manger, with a general pipe of communication to fill them; each trough ſupplying two bullocks. This plan leſſens the expence in ſome degree, and prevents the bullocks from fouling their mangers.

There are individuals in the diſtrict, who have fifty, or more, of one or the other of theſe ſtalls, on their reſpective premiſes.

The number of oxen to a given quantity of hay.

The requiſite attendance.

The ſeaſon of ſtall fatting.

The ſtated times of feeding.

The quantity of cake eaten in a day.

The manner of feeding with hay.

The progreſs of oxen at cakes, and

Putting them from dry meat to graſs,—are ſubjects, which now require to be ſeparately handled.

A. The

A. The NUMBER OF OXEN requiſite to a certain quantity of hay laid up, depends on their ſize, on their ſtate as to forwardneſs, and on the quantity of cake intended to be conſumed with it. In places, where hay is a dear article, cake is the principal food; a ſmall quantity of hay, cut with wheat ſtraw, being given them between the meals of cake; by way of what is termed cleaning their mouths, as well as to correct the over-richneſs of the cake. On the contrary, in this diſtrict, where hay is generally plentiful and cheap, cake becomes, in moſt caſes, ſecondary; hay being conſidered as the principal material of fatting. A man, whoſe practice is extenſive; and whoſe character, as a grazier, is of the firſt caſt; eſtimates a fullſized bullock to conſume, in ſix months, two tons of hay; being allowed, in that time, fifteen hundred weight of oilcake.

B. The requiſite quantity of ATTENDANCE depends, in ſome degree, on circumſtances. The general calculation is one man to about twenty head of oxen:—cutting hay, breaking cake, feeding, watering, littering, and keeping clean, incluſive.

C. The

C. The SEASON of ſtall fatting laſts, in this diſtrict, from November to May; commencing when the aftergraſs is gone, or ſharp weather ſets in; and cloſing with the finiſhing of the bullocks; or when a full bite of ſpring graſs is formed.

D. The STATED MEALS vary with the proportion of hay and cake, and with other circumſtances. In the ordinary practice, three meals of hay; one in the morning,—one at noon,—one in the evening;—and two of cake, one in the forenoon,—the other in the afternoon; are the prevailing number of meals, and the uſual times of feeding.

E. The QUANTITY OF CAKE, which is uſually given each bullock at a meal, is about a quarter of a peck of broken cake;—giving, at the two meals, about half a peck a day.* When it is found requiſite to force them forward for a market, the quantity is ſometimes encreaſed

* The cakes are broken in a large mortar; with a wooden lever-like peſtal, ſhod with iron; or with a beetle, or a ſmall ſledge hammer, in a wooden trough; or are ground in a cider mill; reducing them into fragments of two or three ſquare inches each, down to thoſe of a much ſmaller ſize.

encreaſed to near a peck of broken cake a-day. But in this caſe, it is given them at three or more meals; it being dangerous to cloy them with this ſpecies of food; which is liable to make them ſick;—and, in conſequence, to loathe it, perhaps, for ſeveral days; and, in ſome caſes, to perſevere in refuſing it. In open yards, where cake is ſometimes given to looſe bullocks, this accident not unfrequently happens; the maſter bullocks having an opportunity of eating more than their ſhare; but in ſtalls, where each ox has no more than the quantity which is aſſigned him, this inconveniency can happen through imprudent management, only.

F. The METHOD of feeding with HAY appears in what has paſſed: it is given to them, uncut, two or three times a-day, according to the number of meals of cake, which they have allowed them.

G. The PROGRESS of oxen, and the length of time requiſite to FINISH them, in ſtalls,—depend on the ſpecific quality of the bullocks themſelves; on the ſtate, as to forwardneſs, in which they are taken up; and to the quantity of cake they have allowed. In the ſpecies

ſpecies of grazing now under notice, a large ox, which is bought in lean, is expected to take from ten to twelve months to finiſh him for Smithfield market. If bought in May-June, for inſtance, he has the ſummer's graſs, and lattermath, until, perhaps, the middle of November; when he is put to cake; and ſent off to market at Candlemas, Ladyday, or Mayday, according to the progreſs he has made; or as the chance of a good market may direct.

They are ſeldom, however, kept the whole of the winter in STALLS; the head bullocks, only, being ſtalled at the beginning of the ſeaſon; the reſt having a ſmaller allowance of cake given them, in OPEN YARDS; or, perhaps, have an allowance of hay, only, in the FIELD. As the ſtalled bullocks go to market, their places are ſupplied by the forwardeſt of thoſe, which are more at large.

H. If the laſt-ſtalled bullocks are not finiſhed ſufficiently for market, before ſpring graſs is fit to receive them, they are ſometimes TRANSFERRED FROM THE STALLS TO THE FIELD; and there have been inſtances, in which this was done with conſiderable advantage; though, in general, it does not ſeem to be conſidered as an eligible practice. It is ſufficiently aſcertained, however, that there is no danger in this expedient; and that the cattle, if they do not improve by it, may, at leaſt, be kept from ſinking.

If CAKE be continued to them at GRASS, there can be no doubt of the practice being frequently adviſeable. The markets for fat cattle are generally low at the cloſe of the winterfatting ſeaſon. On the contrary, from that time, until graſs beef be ready, they are moſtly favorable to the ſeller.

7. The MARKET for this ſpecies of fatting cattle is Smithfield; to which they are driven by occaſional drovers, engaged for the purpoſe: there being no ſtationed drovers here, as in Norfolk (ſee NORF: ECON:). The uſual time upon the road is eight days: the diſtance about a hundred miles. They are chiefly (or wholly from *this* diſtrict) conſigned to ſaleſmen. The expence of drift, ſaleſman, toll, &c. is generally about ten ſhillings the head.

8. The PRODUCE of oxen fatted in this manner, will, if valued according to the popu-

lar

lar mode of eſtimation, appear to be very low. They are not expected, during the ten or twelve months fatting, to produce more than *two thirds* of their firſt coſt; while there are many breeds of cattle in this iſland, whoſe individuals would more than *double*, ſome of the ſmaller kinds *treble*, their firſt coſt, in the ſame time, with the ſame keep.

Leſt this fact ſhould be laid hold of, as an argument againſt the Herefordſhire breed of cattle, or the Gloceſterſhire method of fatting them, it may be proper to intimate, that although large cattle conſume, on a par, more food than thoſe of a ſmaller breed; yet it is more than probable, that the diſparity does not keep pace with the difference in their firſt coſts. Thus, it is not probable that an ox of fifteen pounds coſt ſhould conſume as much food as three cows of five pounds, or five Welch heifers of three pounds, each.

The preſent price of this breed of oxen, in working condition, immediately out of the yoke, at ſix year old, is ten to ſixteen pounds each. In the ordinary eſtimation of the country it is expected that theſe oxen ſhould produce, *at graſs*, from three ſhillings to three ſhillings and ſixpence a week; at *hay and cake*, from ſix to ſeven ſhillings; or, the largeſt ſize, at high keep, ſeven ſhillings and ſixpence a week: leaving at the end of ten to twelve months, a groſs produce of ſeven to nine or ten pounds. Twenty five pounds is not an uncommon price for a bullock of this breed in Smithfield market: there has been, I underſtand, ſeveral inſtances in which the Herefordſhire breed of oxen, fatted in this diſtrict, have fetched thirty pounds the ox.

32.

MANAGEMENT OF THE DAIRY.

THE OBJECTS of the dairy, in this diſtrict, are

Calves
Milk butter
Cheeſe
Whey butter
Swine.

But

But previous to an account of the management of each object, individually, it will be proper to notice some subjects, which have a general relation to the whole. These are

1. Dairy-women.
2. Dairy-room.
3. Utensils.
4. Milking.

1. DAIRYWOMEN. The management or immediate superintendance of a large dairy, especially one of which cheese is the principal object, is not a light concern. It requires much thought, and much labour. The whole of the former, and much of the latter, necessarily falls on the immediate superintendant; who, though she may have her assistants, sees or ought to see, herself, to every stage of the business; and performs, or ought to perform, the more difficult operations.

This arduous department is generally undertaken by the MISTRESS OF THE DAIRY; especially on middlesized and small farms. In some cases, an experienced DAIRY MAID is the ostensible manager.

There are three things principally requiſite in the management of a dairy:

Skill,
Induſtry,
Cleanlineſs.

Without the firſt, the two latter may be uſed in vain: and a want of the laſt implies a deficiency in the other two. Cleanlineſs may indeed be conſidered as the *firſt* qualification of a dairywoman; for, without it, ſhe cannot have a fair claim to either ſkill or induſtry.

With reſpect to CLEANLINESS, the Glouceſterſhire dairywomen ſtand unimpeachable. Judging from the dairies I have ſeen, they are much above par, *in reality*;—though not ſo to common *appearance*. A cheeſe dairy is a manufactory—a workſhop—and is, in truth, a place of hard work. That ſtudied *outward neatneſs* which is to be ſeen in the *ſhow dairies* of different diſtricts, and may be in character where *butter* is the only object, would be ſuperfluous in a CHEESE DAIRY. If the room, the utenſils, the dairywoman, and her aſſiſtants be ſufficiently *clean* to give perfect SWEETNESS to the produce, no matter for the *colour*, or the *arrangement*. The *ſcouring wiſp* gives an outward

ward fairneſs; but is frequently an enemy to real cleanlineſs. The *ſcalding bruſh*, only, can give the requiſite SWEETNESS: and I have ſeen it no where more diligently uſed than in Glo-ceſterſhire.

Cleanlineſs implies INDUSTRY. A Gloceſ-terſhire dairywoman is at hard work, from four o'clock in the morning, until bed time.

Her degree of SKILL requires not to be ſpo-ken of here; as it will better appear in the fol-lowing detail, than in any general obſervations which can be made upon it.

2. The DAIRYROOM. The chief peculiarity obſervable in a Gloceſterſhire dairyroom pro-vincially "dairyhouſe"—is that of its gene-rally having an OUTER DOOR, opening into a ſmall yard or garden place; while the dairy of moſt other diſtricts is cooped up in a corner, with only a ſmall window for the admiſſion of air and light; every thing being dragged, in and out, through a number of inner doors, or perhaps rooms or paſſages. But an outer door gives a freer and more general air; and a much better and a more commodious light; beſides rendering the buſineſs of cleanlineſs more eaſy. In the dairy yard there is, or ought to be,

a well;

a well; with proper benches and other conveniences, for waſhing and drying utenſils.

The room, too, is large and commodious: 15 feet by 18 may be conſidered as a middle-ſized dairy. The cheeſe-making and churning are done in the "dairyhouſe": ſo that the entire buſineſs is collected into as narrow a compaſs as may be: a circumſtance of ſome importance, in a large dairy; and, in a ſmall one, the advantage is proportional. The *floor* is generally laid with ſtone. The *ſhelves* are moſtly of elm, or aſh.

With reſpect to ASPECT, the outer door, when well placed, opens near the northeaſt or the northweſt corner: the window on the north ſide: the inner door, on the ſouth-ſide, opening into the kitchen.

A dairyroom on this plan is, perhaps, as commodious as art can render it.

3. UTENSILS. A detail of the furniture of a dairy may appear unintereſting; and, by ſome readers, be thought unneceſſary. It would be difficult, however, to give a minute account of the method of carrying on the *manufacture*, without deſcribing the *tools* in uſe: a deſcription of them is little more than a definition

tion of technical terms. Perſpicuity requires it.

1. *Milking pail.* The ſhape nearly that of a buſhel. But formed of ſtaves and hoops; with *one* "handle ſtave" riſing three or four inches above the rim. (The Yorkſhire *ſkeel* with one handel.) The diameter about fifteen inches; the depth about ten inches. Staves oak—hoops (broad and cloſe) aſh.

2. *Milk cooler*; provincially "cheeſe cowl." —This is a large ſtrong wooden veſſel, proportioned in ſize to the number of cows. From eighteen inches, to two feet deep:—and from two to three feet diameter. Two oppoſite ſtaves riſe above the reſt: the head of each having a hole in it, large enough to admit a pole; for the purpoſe of moving it, or carrying it on men's ſhoulders; anſwering the purpoſe, occaſionally, of what in ſome diſtricts is called a *bearing tub*; in others a *cowl.*

3. *Strainer; or milk ſieve.* Made ſieve-form: twelve or fourteen inches diameter: five or ſix inches deep: ſome with hair bottoms: others have cloth bottoms; which are taken out every day to waſh. A frond or leaf of fern is

is frequently placed at the bottom of the ſieve to prevent the milk from flying over.

4. *Sieve holder*; provincially "cheeſe ladder."—This is laid acroſs the cooler to place the *milk ſieve* or ſtrainer upon. It has here a valuable ſingularity of conſtruction: at one end are two croſs bars about three inches apart. This vacancy admitting one "ear" or handle of the cooler, the ladder is kept ſecurely in its place. The wood, aſh.

5. *Lading diſh*. The uſual ſhape but large; near a foot diameter.

6. *Pail bruſhes*. Common hard bruſhes; furniſhed with briſtles at the end, to clean out the angles of the veſſels more effectually. Utenſils, or rather tools, which no dairy ought to be without. Yet in many diſtricts of the kingdom their uſes are unknown.

7. *Pail-ſtake*. A ſimple contrivance; or rather a *thought*; which one would imagine, no perſon, having dairy utenſils to dry, could miſs: yet it appears to have been hit upon in this country only. In other diſtricts I ſee milking pails, &c. placed upon benches, or upon walls, to dry; where they are liable to be blown down by the wind, or thrown down and burſt

burſt by other means. Here, a bough, furniſhed with many branchlets, is fixed with its but-end in the ground, in the dairy yard. The branchlets being lopped, of a due length, each ſtump becomes a peg to hang a pail upon or other utenſil.

8. " *Skeels.*"—-Theſe are broad ſhallow veſſels; principally for the purpoſe of ſetting milk in, to ſtand for cream: made in the tub manner, with ſtaves and hoops, and two ſtave handles: of various ſizes, from eighteen inches to two feet and a half diameter; and from five to ſeven inches deep. Staves oak; hoops (broad and cloſe) aſh.

9. *Skimming diſhes.* If of wood, very thin. But chiefly of *tin.* About eight inches diameter; and five eights of an inch deep.

10. *Cream jars.* Cream is chiefly preſerved in earthen jars of a middle ſize.

11. " *Cream ſlice.*" A wooden knife; ſome what in the ſhape of a table knife. Length 12 or 14 inches.

12. *Churns.* Upright and barrel churns are in uſe. The barrel churn with one fixt and one looſe handle. Noway excellent in their conſtruction. Butter is here a *ſecondary* object

object. The Yorkshire churn is preferable: but this might be expected: there butter is the *primary* object of the dairy.

13. *Butter board, and trowel.* A broad board and a wooden spatula, used in "printing" the butter.

14. *Butter prints.* The halfpound print four inches diameter.

15. *Cheese knife.* A wooden handle, four or five inches long,—furnished with two, or three iron blades, twelve inches long, and one inch broad, at the handle, down to about three quarters of an inch at the point; with two blunt edges, rounded at the point, like an ivory paper-knife. The distance between the blades, which are very thin, and ranged with their flat sides toward each other, about an inch.

16. *Cheese vats.* From fifteen to fifteen and a half inches diameter; and from one and a half inch to two inches deep. The wood invariably elm. Some with, but many without holes.

17. *Cheese cloths.* Made of thin gauze-like linnen cloth. The size varies in different dairies.

18. *Cheese-*

18. *Cheeſe preſs.* The conſtruction various. Sometimes ſingle; but, in large dairies, generally double. The preſſure is moſtly given by a dead weight, raiſed by a roller, and falling perpendicularly on the cheeſe. In the upper vale, they are chiefly of ſtone. The dimenſions of one of a ſuperior weight are twenty two inches ſquare, by two feet two inches long; containing 12,584 cubical inches of freeſtone; weighing (on the ſuppoſition, that its ſpecific gravity is an ounce and a half to an inch) ſomewhat more than half a ton.

But, by an accurate experiment, I found, that a cubical inch of ſimilar ſtone (freeſtone of the Cotſwold cliffs) weighs only 500 grains. Therefore, calculating the pound averdupois at 7,000 grains troy, the ſtone under notice weighs eight hundredweight.

The dimenſions of other three (all of the ſame ſize and in the ſame dairy) are 20 inches wide, by 14 deep, and two feet four inches long: containing 7,840 cubical inches of Cotſwold freeſtone: conſequently, weigh no more than five hundredweight each.

Theſe are of the *old conſtruction*; which is *very* ſimple. In the center is fixt a wooden

ſkrew,

ſkrew, riſing three or four feet perpendicularly above the ſtone; paſſing through a hole in a croſs beam, reſting on the cheeks of the preſs. Above this croſs-piece is worked a looſe nut, made out of a piece of wood, eighteen inches to two feet long, and of a diameter proportioned to the ſize of the worm. Each end is reduced to the ſize of a handle; and with this two-handled nut the ſtone is raiſed and lowered. The perpendicularity of the ſkrew keeps the baſe of the ſtone horizontal; and to keep it more ſteady in its place, it is notched at each end about an inch deep, to admit the cheeks, or ſlips nailed on the inner ſides of them, for that purpoſe.

4. Milking. The hours of milking are here early: about five in the morning, and four in the evening; in order to give due time for finiſhing the requiſite buſineſs of the dairy, before bed-time.

Where a large dairy of cows are kept, the whole family (excepting thoſe who have the care of the teams) muſter to milking. An indoor ſervant, by the name of a "milking man" is generally kept, in the larger dairies, for the purpoſe of milking, churning, and otherwiſe

otherwiſe aſſiſting in the buſineſs of the dairy: he has the care of the cows and the cow-grounds; and is conſidered as a principal ſervant.

When the "COWGROUND" lies near the houſe, the cows are generally brought into the yard, or other ſmall incloſure: if the paſture lie at a diſtance, the pails are always carried to the cows. Alſo if the ground be very wet, and poach with the cows travelling over it, judicious dairymen have the pails carried to them. In more than one inſtance, I have ſeen a horſe and barrel-cart employed, to take the milk from a diſtant meadow or cowground to the dairyhouſe.

The practice is to milk the cows unfettered; and to uſe ſquare-topped, four-legged ſtools; reſting one edge of the bottom of the large pail, here in uſe, againſt two legs of the ſtool. Hence the conveniency of its form.

The management of the particular OBJECTS of the dairy now require attention.

I. CALVES. Theſe, being the firſt produce, and as it were the origin of dairies, require to be firſt noticed.

The REARING OF CALVES has been already ſpoken of, in p. 255. The method of fatting them remains to be mentioned in this place.

The FATTING OF CALVES being, here, a *ſubordinate* object of the dairy, no very accurate ideas on the ſubject muſt be expected: the late-dropt calves are an encumbrance on cheeſmaking, the primary object, and are of courſe got rid of as ſoon as poſſible. One ſingularity of management, however, requires to be noticed.

Calves, whether for rearing or fatting, are ſeldom ſuffered to *ſuck* more than two or three days; ſometimes they are put to the *pail*, as ſoon as they are dropt; the milk being, I believe, pretty univerſally paſſed through the *kettle*; and given to the calves *warmer* than it comes from the cow. On the increaſed heat of the milk, the advantage of this *unnatural* mode of fatting is *here* thought principally to hinge. See YORK: ECON: ii, 295, on this ſubject.

II. MILK BUTTER. In the upper vale, milk butter forms a conſiderable object of the dairy: not only in the ſpring, while calves are rearing, before cheeſmaking commences; but

but during ſummer: owing to the SPECIES OF CHEESE, which is univerſally made here; and which is, I believe, peculiar to the vale of Glocester. It is called "two-meal cheeſe." The evening's meal is ſet for cream; and, being ſkimmed in the morning, is added to the morning's meal, neat from the cow.

The method of making butter in this diſtrict, therefore, merits a deſcription in detail; eſpecially as GLOCESTER BUTTER,—which is diſtributed, by huckſters, to diſtant parts of the country, bears a ſuperior character. The ſtages of the art are,—

1. Setting the milk.
2. Preſerving the cream.
3. Churning.
4. Making up the butter.
5. Markets.

1. SETTING THE MILK. This I have ſeen done in different ways: every diſtrict exhibits good and bad management,—in almoſt every department of rural affairs. The beſt method of ſetting milk in this country, which I have ſeen, and which may, I believe, be called the beſt practice of the diſtrict, is this.

The milk having remained in the cooler, a time, proportioned to the heat of the weather; ſo as to lower it to about 80° of Farenheit's thermometer; it is parcelled out in "ſkeels:" or, if theſe are not ſufficiently numerous to receive it, in any other dairy veſſel;—leaving, perhaps, a part of it in the cooler*; dividing it in ſuch a manner, as to leave it about an *inch deep*, in each veſſel: the dairywoman meaſuring the depth, by the joint of her finger; and carefully placing the veſſels level; ſo that one ſide be not left deeper than the other. The prevailing rule is *to ſet it as ſhallow as it can be conveniently ſkimmed*; under a conviction, that the ſhallower it is ſet, the more cream will riſe, from a given quantity of milk. An inch and a half is the ordinary depth; but, in the practice I am more particularly regiſtering, the dairywoman has dexterity of finger ſufficient to ſkim it at an inch deep. This, however, could not be done without the aſſiſtance of a *tin ſkimming diſh*; which being thinner,

* MILK-LEADS are not common in this diſtrict. I have, nevertheleſs, ſeen ſome very old ones in uſe: a circumſtantial evidence, that their uſe has been long *known* in this diſtrict.

thinner, gathers up the cream cleaner, than a wooden one; but requires a more ſteady hand to guide it.

2. PRESERVING THE CREAM. Earthern jars are the common receptacles of cream.—In theſe it is *ſtirred* ſeveral times a day, with the "cream ſlice;" but ſeems to be *ſhifted* leſs frequently, here, than in ſome other dairy countries. Cream, here, has a peculiar propenſity to become "curdy;" loſing its liquid ſtate; requiring ſome ſtrength of hand to ſtir it; ariſing probably, from its ſuperior richneſs *

3. CHURNING. In the practice, which I more particularly attended to, the buſineſs of churning is conducted in this manner:—If the weather be hot, the churn is previouſly cooled with cold water; and, if wanted, cold water is likewiſe put into the churn among the cream. On the contrary, if the weather be cold, the churn is warmed with ſcalding water;

* COLOURING BUTTER. In autumn, when butter generally becomes pale and tallow-like, the cream is not unfrequently *coloured*, before it be put into the churn. The material of colouring is the ſame as that uſed in the colouring of cheeſe; which will be ſpoken of in the next article. The method of uſing it, however, is ſomewhat different.

water; and, if wanted, hot water is put into the churn; which, perhaps, in ſevere weather, is placed near the fire, during the operation.

The cream of the vale is very liable to riſe in the churn; owing, probably, to its peculiar richneſs. Under this circumſtance, part of it is taken out; and, when that which is left in the churn is gone down again, the part taken out is re-added.

The mouth of the churn is ſecured with butter, preſſed plaſterwiſe into the joints.—This is thought to be leſs troubleſome than a cloth.

The *breaking* is here carefully attended to. It is conſidered as very injurious to heat the butter in the churn.

4. Making up butter. In making up butter, the firſt buſineſs is to prepare the ſeveral utenſils employed in the operation.—Here they conſiſt of the "butter ſkeel"—the "butter board"—the "print" and "trowell." The preparation required is to prevent the butter from hanging to the wood. It is here done with ſcalding water, and *ſalt*, bruſhed into the wood while moiſt and hot, with

with a ſoft thick-ſet bruſh: either putting the ſalt upon the bruſh, or duſting it over the utenſil; which, being ſalted, is immediately plunged into cold water. The dairywoman's hands are prepared in a ſimilar manner.

I will give the minutiæ of this operation, as performed by a moſt excellent dairywoman; whoſe butter ſeldom fails of being of the firſt quality. They differ from thoſe, which I have already given;* and are, probably, the beſt which I may have an opportunity of obſerving; and probably the laſt, upon which I may beſtow the tedioufneſs of regiſtering.

The butter being taken out of the churn, and placed in the "ſkeel," with a quantity of cold clear water,—the dairywoman breaks off a lump, (ſomewhat more than a pound) and, with one hand, kneads it in the water, *with the fingers ſpread widely abroad*; cloſing them at intervals; thereby breaking the butter moſt effectually; conſequently giving the contained milk an opportunity of eſcaping. Every time the fingers are cloſed, the lump is rolled on the bottom of the ſkeel; the hand ſhifted, taking

* See NORF: ECON: MIN: 109.

taking the lump the contrary way; and worked as before. This being ſeveral times repeated, the firſt roll is placed upon the butter board, and a freſh lump broken off.

The whole being gone over in this manner, the milky water is poured out (into the tub of buttermilk*) the ſkeel waſhed, and ſomewhat more than half the butter ſpread thinly and evenly, but *roughly*, over the bottom of it. SALT is then duſted upon this rough ſurface; the remaining lumps of butter ſpread over the ſalt; and over the whole another portion of ſalt is ſtrewed.

The dairywoman now rolls the whole into one lump; which ſhe immediately breaks down with the palm of her hand; the fingers expanded as before; forcing the butter from her; cloſing the fingers partially at every ſtroke;

* BUTTER MILK is here acidulated for the hogs; being mixed among the whey, which is alſo given to the hogs ſtale and ſour: not, I believe, as a matter of choice, which is ſtudied; but as a matter of conveniency.

In winter, when butter milk is ſweet, it is ſometimes run, among other milk, for "family cheeſe;" and affords a conſiderable quantity of curd; but it makes what is called a "bitter meſs," and the running of it, is, I underderſtand, conſidered as a mean ſpecies of economy.

ſtroke; thereby leaving it at the bottom of the ſkeel *exceedingly rough.*

Over this rugged ſurface freſh water is poured; the butter rolled up again into one large lump; again broken down in the manner laſt-deſcribed: and again formed into one large roll.—This is at length broken into pound lumps; and kneaded in the water, as in the firſt inſtance.

The butter is now a ſecond time upon the butter board (over which water is always thrown before the lumps be placed upon it) and the ſkeel being emptied of the briney water, the lumps are ſeparately kneaded (with one hand) on the bottom of it, *dry*; and ſet in ſhort rolls, againſt the ſide of the ſkeel.

The butter ſcales are then taken out of the ſalt water, which was poured out of the ſkeel, and in which they have been immerſed during the laſt operation, and evenly balanced with butter; the lumps divided; and weighed in *half-pound pieces*: which are again returned into the ſkeel; or, for want of room, are placed upon the board.

This being effected, the lumps are prepared for printing; by kneading them, dry, at the bottom

bottom of the ſkeel; and moulding each into a conical form; with the palm of the hand; and with the fingers joined, and ſet at right angle to the palm. The point of the cone-like lump thus formed, being placed in the center of the print, the baſe is preſſed down, until the ſurface of the print be covered. What preſſes over, at the edges, is collected, (by running the finger round the print,) and put upon the intended bottom of the pat. The ſides are finally ſmoothed with the trowel; the pat with the print ſet upon the butter board; and the print taken off: leaving the pat about 4 inches diameter and about 1½ inch thick. *

If

* BUTTER GAUGE. A cubical inch of well wrought butter weighed 230 grains; or ſomewhat more than half an ounce averdupois. Therefore a pound averdupois of well wrought butter contains ſomewhat more than thirty cubical inches (30. 4.) And the ſtandard pound of this diſtrict (18 oz:) meaſures more than thirty four inches (34. 25.) The half pound ſomewhat more than ſeventeen inches. Hence a half pound print or pat of butter exactly four inches in diameter ought (if well worked and honeſtly weighed) to meaſure exactly 1. 3628 inches in depth.

A meaſure, of ſome regular figure, as a cube, accurately formed, on theſe principles, would be the beſt ſtandard for a

market

If the print does not "loose" freely, the hand is placed, carefully and firmly, againſt the ſide of the pat; thereby gaining a degree of purchaſe to pull againſt. If the butter be found to adhere in any degree to the wood, the print is ſcalded, ſalted and bruſhed, until it looſen freely; without the indelicacy of *blowing* in the manner practiſed in moſt places. The pats remain ſome length of time, generally one night, upon the board to ſtiffen; and, in the morning, are placed in cold water, previous to their being put into the baſkets, in which they are carried to market.

5. MARKETS. The butter markets of the upper vale are chiefly *Glocester*, *Cheltenham*, *Tewkeſbury*, and *Eveſham*. That of Glocester is the largeſt and the *neateſt* butter-market I have anywhere obſerved. The butter is all brought in half-pound pats or prints, packed

market inqueſt; as it would not only check the weight; but the purity of the butter alſo: provided due care were obſerved in preſſing it cloſely into the gauge; thereby freeing it from the redundant moiſture, which dairy-women, who are ſkilfull and honeſt, extract before they take it to market; but which the ſlovenly and the deſigning ſell at the price of butter. See NORFOLK, MIN: 109.

packed up in ſquare baſkets, in a manner which merits deſcription.

The baſkets are invariably of one form: long-ſquare; with a bow-handle acroſs the middle; and with two lids, hingeing upon a croſs piece under the bow. The dimenſions of an ordinary baſket are 18 by 14 inches within; and about 10 inches deep. This baſket holds twelve prints (four by three) in one layer or tire. When the butter is firm, three layers or 18 lb. are put in each baſket; when ſoft two tires or 12 lb. One of a larger ſize meaſures 18 by 23 inches within; carrying twenty half pounds in each tire; or 30 lb. in the three tires. The baſket is put into a kind of open wallet; with generally a ſmaller baſket or other counterpois at the oppoſite end of the wallet; which being ſtrapt tightly to the ſaddle (judiciouſly made for this purpoſe) with the heavy end on the off ſide of the horſe, the dairymaid mounts, and, with her own weight, preſerves the balance. The baſket being laſhed on in ſuch a manner as to ride perfectly level, the prints are preſerved from bruiſing.

In ſummer, the butter is invariably packed in green leaves: generally in what the dairy-women call "butter leaves": namely the leaves of the *Atriplex hortenſis*, or garden orach; which dairywomen in general ſow in their gardens, annually, for this purpoſe. They are ſufficiently large; of a fine texture; and a delicate pale-green colour. For want of theſe, vine leaves, and thoſe of kidney-beans &c. are uſed.

In packing a butter baſket, the bottom is bedded with a thick cloth, folded two or three times. On this is ſpread a fine thin gauze-like cloth, which has been dipped in cold water; and on this is placed the prints; with a large leaf beneath, and a ſmaller upon the center of each. The bottom tire adjuſted, a fold of the cloth is ſpread over it, and another tire ſet in, in a ſimilar manner. At market, the cloth is removed; and the prints, partially covered with leaves, ſhown in all their neatneſs. The leaves are uſeful as well as pleaſing to the eye. They ſerve as guards to the prints. The butter is taken out of the baſket, as well as put in to it, without being touched, or the prints disfigured.

III. Cheese.

III. CHEESE. The art of making GLOCESTERSHIRE CHEESE was originally one of the principal objects which induced me to make choice of Glocestershire as a STATION. My practice in Norfolk* had shown me that, in the quality of cheese, although much may depend upon SOIL and HERBAGE, much is certainly due to MANAGEMENT.

GLOCESTERSHIRE has long been celebrated for its excellency in this art: and where shall we study an art with so much propriety as in the place where it excels? It may be proper to add, that altho' my own experience had not led me to perfection, it had sufficiently enabled me to make accurate observations on the practices of others. An ANALYTICAL ARRANGEMENT, of the several departments and stages of the art, was a guard against my suffering any material part to escape my notice; and the THERMOMETER a certain guide in those difficult passages, in which an accuracy of judgement, is more peculiarly requisite.

* See RURAL ECONOMY OF NORFOLK. MIN: 108.

The

The objects of my attention have been

Soils	Management of the curd
Water	Management of the cheese
Herbage	Defects and Excellencies
Cows	Markets
Quality of milk	Produce.
Colouring	
Rennets	
Method of running	

The management of the two vales under survey differ in one most material article;—the *quality* of the milk. In the lower vale, the milk is run neat from the cow (or nearly so). In the upper vale, it has been already said, the prevailing practice is to set the evening's meal for cream; in the morning to skim it; and then to add it to the new milk of the morning's meal. The cheese made from this mixture is termed "TWO-MEAL CHEESE": that from the neat milk, "one-meal cheese" or "BEST MAKING."

Besides this difference in produce, or SPECIES OF CHEESE, there are other differences in the practices of the two vales. It will therefore be proper to register them separately; lest by mixing them, the perspicuity, which is requisite

requiſite in deſcribing the minutiæ of an art ſo complex and difficult as this under conſideration, ſhould be deſtroyed.

Of the UPPER VALE the *ſoil*, the *herbage*, and the *cow* have been already mentioned: the ſubjects which remain to be noticed in this place are

1. The ſeaſon of making
2. The quality of the milk
3. Colouring
4. Rennets
5. Running
6. Management of the curd
7. Management of the cheeſe
8. Markets.

1. THE SEASON OF MAKING. From the beginning of May to the latter end of October, including ſeven months, may be conſidered as the ſeaſon of cheeſmaking, in this diſtrict.

2. THE QUALITY OF THE MILK. The mixture for twomeal cheeſe has been mentioned, in general terms, to be one part ſkim milk (namely milk which has ſtood *one* meal for cream) and one part new milk, *neat* from the cow. But *this* is ſeldom, I apprehend, ſtrictly the caſe. A little *fraud* is, I am afraid, generally

generally practised. A greater or less proportion of the morning's meal is set for cream, and returned the next morning to the cheese cowl,—*robbed* of its better part. This is a trick played upon the cheese factor: but he being aware of the practice, little advantage, probably, is got by it. However, where the soil is superiorly rich, a small proportion may be "kept out", and the cheese, nevertheless, be of a *fair* quality.

3. COLOURING. This is another *deception* which has long been practised by the Glocestershire dairywomen; and which, heretofore, probably, they practised exclusively. The colouring of cheese, however, is now become a practice in other districts.

The practice has no doubt arisen from the Glocestershire dairywomen's having observed, that, on some soils, and in some seasons, cheese naturally acquires a yellow colour; and such cheese having been found to bear a better price, (either from its intrinsic quality, or because it pleased the eye better) than cheese of a paler colour, they set about *counterfeiting nature*; and in the outset, no doubt, found their end in it.

There is ſome difficulty, however, in this as in other caſes, to copy nature exactly. Much depends on the material; and ſomething on the method of uſing it. If the colouring material be improperly choſen, or injudiciouſly uſed, the colour appears in ſtreaks, and inſtead of pleaſing the eye, offends it. On the contrary, with a ſuitable material, properly uſed, the artifice may be rendered undetectable.

The material which has at length obtained univerſal eſteem; and which, I believe, is now, almoſt invariably uſed; is a preparation of ANNOTTA; a drug, the produce of Spaniſh America. It is brought to England (for the the uſe of the dyers principally I believe) under the appearance of an earthy clay-like ſubſtance; but is well known to be a vegetable production. †

It

† ANNOTTA is the produce of *Bixa Orellana* of Linneus. Miller deſcribes the plant and its propagation. It is a talliſh ſhrub, ſomewhat reſembling the lilac. The colouring material is the pulp of the fruit; among which the ſeeds are bedded, in a manner ſomewhat ſimilar to thoſe of the roſe, in the pulp of the hep. It is a native of the Weſt Indies, and the warmer parts of America: Annotta Bay in Jamaica takes

It has been tried as a colouring of cheeſe in its genuine ſtate; but without ſucceſs. The PREPARATION, which is here uſed, is made by druggiſts both in London and in the country; and is ſold at the ſhops in Gloceſter, and other towns in the diſtrict, in rolls or knobs of three or four ounces each. In colour and contexture it is not unlike well burnt red brick. But it varies in appearance and goodneſs: the hardeſt and cloſeſt is eſteemed the beſt. *

The method of uſing it is this. A piece of the preparation is rubbed againſt a hard ſmooth even-faced pebble, or other ſtone; the pieces being previouſly wetted with milk, to forward the levigation, and to collect the particles as they are looſened. For this purpoſe a diſh of milk is generally placed upon the

takes its name from this ſhrub. The pigment, it is ſaid, was formerly collected in Jamaica: but has of later years been brought there (in ſeroons, or bags made of undreſſed hides) from the Spaniſh ſettlements.

* With reſpect to the *crime* of colouring cheeſe, I ſay nothing in this place: as I ſhall have a better opportunity of ſpeaking of it, when the VALE OF BERKELEY becomes the ſubject of notice.

the cheeſe-ladder; and as the ſtone becomes loaded with levigated matter the pieces are dipped in the milk from time to time; until the milk in the diſh appear (from daily practice) to be ſufficiently coloured.

The ſtone and the "colouring" being waſhed clean in the milk, it is ſtirred briſkly about in the diſh; and, having ſtood a few minutes for the unſuſpended particles of colouring to ſettle, is returned into the cheeſe-cowl; pouring it off gently, ſo as to leave any ſediment which may have fallen down, in the bottom of the diſh. The grounds are then rubbed with the finger on the bottom of the diſh, and freſh milk added; until all the finer particles be *ſuſpended*: and in this the ſkill in colouring principally conſiſts. If any fragments have broken off in the operation, they remain at the bottom of the diſh: hence the ſuperiority of a hard cloſely textured material, which will not break off or crumble in rubbing.

The price of annotta is about ten pence an ounce; which will colour about twenty thin cheeſes (10 or 12 pounds each). The colouring therefore coſts about a halfpenny a cheeſe.

4. RENNETS.

4. Rennets. Rennets are here learnedly ſpoken of,—by thoſe who are ſuperficially acquainted with their uſe. Experienced dairywomen, however, ſpeak modeſtly on the ſubject: what they principally expect from rennet is the *coagulation* of their milk; having little faith in its being able to *correct* any evil quality which the milk may be poſſeſſed of.

The univerſal *baſis* is the ſtomach of a calf; provincially a "vell"; from which an extract is drawn, in various ways; according to the judgement or *belief* of the dairywoman.

1. The preparation of the vell;—namely the cleanſing and pickling is generally done to their hands. Beſides the internal ſupply, London and Ireland furniſh this country with great numbers of vells; which are brought in caſks, in pickle, and ſold by the grocers and other ſhopkeepers. The price of Engliſh vells about ſixpence a piece, of Iriſh about fourpence; theſe being comparatively ſmall. *

2. Preparation of the rennet. In the dairy which I more particularly attended

* Some of them, it ſeems, are *ſuſpected* to be "lambs vells."

to in the upper vale, the rennet underwent no *eſtabliſhed* mode of preparation. The *prevailing* method is this: ſome *whey*, being ſalted, until it will bear an egg, is ſuffered to ſtand all night to purge itſelf: in the morning it is ſkimmed and racked off clear: to this is added an equal quantity of *water-brine*, and into this briney mixture is put ſome ſweet briar, thyme, hyſſop, or other "ſweet herbs"; alſo a little black pepper, ſalt petre &c.; tying the herbs in bunches, and letting them remain in the brine a few days. Into about ſix quarts of this liquor, four Engliſh vells, or a proportionate number of Iriſh ones, are put; and having lain in it three or four days, the rennet is fit for uſe. No part of the preparation is boiled, or even heated: and frequently no other preparation whatever is uſed, than that of ſteeping the vells in cold ſalt and water. Indeed, in another dairy, which I had an opportunity of obſerving in the upper vale, no other mode of preparation was uſed; and few, if any, dairies make better cheeſe: I ſpeak from my own knowledge.

Therefore, from the evidence which I have collected in the upper vale it appears that, provided

provided the *vells* be duly *prepared*—be thoroughly cleanſed and cured—no ſubſequent preparation of *rennet* is neceſſary. Nevertheleſs, were I to recommend a practice in this caſe, it would be that of doing away the natural *faint* flavor of the vells, by ſome aromatic infuſion. But I ſhould prefer *ſpices* to *herbs* for this purpoſe.

5. RUNNING. In this, as in every other ſtage and department of cheeſmaking there are *ſhades of difference*, in the practices of different dairywomen. No two conduct the buſineſs exactly alike; nor is the practice of any individual uniform. There are, at preſent, no fixed principles to go by. Every thing is left to the deciſion of the ſenſes; uncertain guides. Nevertheleſs, *practice*, carried on with attention, and aſſiſted by good natural abilities, will do much; though it cannot, alone, attain that degree of perfection, which, when joined with *ſcience*, it is capable of reaching.

Th emiſtreſs of the dairy, whoſe practice I am more particularly regiſtering, has both natural and acquired advantages, which render her dairy, though not of the firſt magnitude,

 a proper

a proper ſubject of ſtudy. Her father was poſſeſſed of the beſt breed of cows in the vale, and was one of the largeſt dairy farmers in it. Her mother, the firſt among its dairy-women; and herſelf poſſeſſed of that *natural cleverneſs*, without which no woman, let her *education* be what it may, can conduct, with any degree of ſuperiority, the buſineſs of a cheeſe dairy.

In giving a detail of my own practice in Norfolk, I mentioned ſome known principles of coagulation; as well as ſome received opinions of dairywomen, reſpecting the nature of this proceſs. The ſame opinions are held in this diſtrict; in which ſome other received ideas prevail: namely, that the quantity of curd is in proportion to the length of time of coagulation: there being "the leaſt curd when longeſt in coming."

That ſetting the milk hot, inclines the cheeſe to "heave": (a defect which will be ſpoken to hereafter.)

And that lowering the heat of the milk with cold water (when made too hot) has a ſimilar effect.

To give fome idea of the practice of the upper vale, in this moft delicate ftage of the art, I will detail the obfervations made, during five fucceffive mornings, in the dairy which has been fpoken of.

Tuefday, 2 *September*, 1783. The quality of the milk, that which has been defcribed. Part of the fkim milk added cold; — part warmed in a kettle over the fire, to raife the whole to a due degree of heat. Coloured in the manner defcribed. An eftimated fufficiency of runnet added. The whole ftirred and mixed evenly together. The exact heat of the mixture 85° of Farenheit's thermometer. The morning clofe and warm, with fome thunder. The cheefe cowl covered;— but placed near an open door. The curd, neverthelefs, came in lefs than forty minutes: much fooner than expected: owing probably to the peculiar ftate of the air. The retained heat of the curd and whey, when broken up and mixed evenly together, 82°. The curd deemed too tough and hard; though much the tendereft curd I have obferved.

Wednefday, 3 *September*. The morning moderately cool. The heat of the milk when

fet

ſet 83½°. The cowl partially covered, and expoſed to the outward air as before. Came in an hour and a quarter. The heat of the curd and whey mixed evenly together 80°. But at the top, before mixing, only 77°. The curd extremely delicate, and eſteemed of a good quality.

Thurſday, 4 *September*. The morning cool —a ſlight froſt. The milk heated this morning to 88°. The cowl more cloſely covered; and the door ſhut part of the time. Set at half paſt ſix: began to come at half after ſeven: but not ſufficiently hard, to be broken up, until eight o'clock:—an hour and a half. The whey, when mixt, exactly 80°! The curd exceedingly delicate.

Thus it ſhould ſeem, that it is not the heat of the milk when it is run; but the heat of the whey, when the curd is ſufficiently coagulated, which gives the quality of the curd. My own practice led me to the ſame idea. And the Gloceſterſhire dairywomen, by their practice, ſeem fully aware of the fact. As autumn advances, the heat of the milk is increaſed. And accordingly as the given morning

ing happens to be warm or cool, the degree of warmth of the milk is varied.

Friday, 5 September. This morning, tho' mild, the curd came exactly at 80°! What an accuracy of judgement here appears to be displayed! Let the state of the air be what it will, we find the heat of the whey, when the curd is sufficiently coagulated, exactly 80°. and this, without the assistance of a thermometer, or any other artificial help. But what will not daily practice, natural good sense, and minute attention accomplish.

Saturday, 6 September. This morning the curd came too quick. The heat of the whey (after the curd had been broken and was settled) full 85°! The curd "much tougher and harder than it should be." Here we have a proof of the inaccuracy of the senses; and of the insufficiency of the natural judgement in the art under consideration: it may frequently *prove to be right*; but never can be *certain*. Some scientific helps are evidently necessary to UNIFORM SUCCESS.

6. THE

6. THE MANAGEMENT OF THE CURD.—This ſtage of the proceſs has five diſtinct operations belonging to it.

1. Breaking.
2. Gathering.
3. Scalding.
4. Vatting.
5. Preſerving ſpare curd.

1. *Breaking*. Here new ideas pour in.—The curd, while ſuſpended in the whey, is never touched with the hands*. The curd is broken, or rather cut, with the triple "cheeſe knife," which has been deſcribed. This mode of ſeparating the curd and whey, tho' not univerſal, appears to be highly eligible: the intention of it is that of "keeping the fat in the cheeſe:" a matter which, in the manufacture of two-meal cheeſe, is of the firſt conſideration. The opera tion is performed in this manner.

The knife is firſt drawn its full depth acroſs cowl in two or three places; and likewiſe round

* In another dairy, however, whoſe manager ranks high among dairywomen, the curd is broken with the hands alone; in the manner deſcribed in NORF: ECON:

round by the ſides; in order to give the whey an opportunity of eſcaping as clear as may be Having ſtood five or ten minutes, the knife is more freely uſed: drawing it briſkly in every direction, until the upper part of the curd be cut into ſmall checquers. The bottom is then ſtirred up with the diſh, in the left hand; and, while the lumps are ſuſpended in the whey, they are cut with the knife, in the right: thus continuing to ſtir up the curd with the diſh, and ſeparate the lumps with the knife, until not a lump larger than a bean is ſeen to riſe to the ſurface.

2. *Gathering*. The curd having been allowed about half an hour to ſettle in, the whey is laded off, with the diſh; paſſing it through a hair ſieve into ſome other veſſel.

The principal part of the whey being laded off, the curd is drawn to one ſide of the cowl, and preſſed hard with the bottom of the diſh: the ſkirts and edges cut off with a common knife, and the cuttings laid upon the principal maſs; which is carried round the tub, among the remaining whey, to gather up the ſcattered fragments that lie among it. The whole being collected, the whey is all

all laded or poured off, and the curd left in one maſs, at the bottom of the cowl.

3. *Scalding.* It is, I believe, the invariable practice of the dairywomen of Glocestershire, to *ſcald the curd**. This accounts for their running the milk ſo comparatively cool. Were the delicate cool-run curd of this diſtrict to be made into cheeſe, without previouſly ſcalding, the cheeſes made from it would require an inconvenient length of time to fit them for market.

The method of ſcalding the curd, here, varies from that mentioned in the Economy of Norfolk. There it was ſcalded in the maſs; pouring hot water over the ſurface, as it lay at the bottom of the cheeſe-tub: but, here, the maſs is broken; firſt by cutting it into ſquare pieces with a common knife; and then reducing it, with the triple knife, into ſmall fragments; moſtly as ſmall as peas: none of them is left larger than a walnut: and among theſe fragments the "ſcalding ſtuff" is thrown; ſtirring them briſkly about; thereby effectually mixing them together; and, of courſe, ſcalding

* See NORF: ECON:

ſcalding the whole as effectually, and as evenly, as this method of ſcalding will admit of.

The *liquid* made uſe of here, for ſcalding curd, varies in different dairies. Some dairywomen ſcald with *whey*; violently objecting to water; while others uſe *water*; objecting with equal obſtinacy to whey: while dairywomen in general, I believe, mix the two together*.

The *quantity* is in proportion to the quantity of curd: enough to float the curd; and make the mixture eaſy to be ſtirred about with the diſh.

Part of it is heated to near boiling heat; and this lowered with cold liquid TO A HEAT PROPORTIONED TO THE STATE OF THE CURD: ſoft curd is ſcalded with hot; hard curd with cooler liquid.

In ſcalding, therefore, the dairywoman has a remedy for any misjudgement her ſenſe of feeling may have led her into, in the ſtage of coagulation: let the curd come too ſoft or too hard, ſhe can bring it to the deſired texture, by the heat of the ſcalding liquid. And here

* It ſeems to be underſtood, that different grounds require different kinds of ſcalding liquor.

here ſeems to hinge, principally, the ſuperior ſkill of the Glouceſterſhire dairywoman: by running the milk cool, ſhe can, in ſcalding, correct any error, which has been committed in running.

Saturday, 6 *September*. This morning, the curd being too tough, the *whey* was uſed cooler than it was yeſterday morning, when the curd was ſufficiently tender. (See page 299.) Yeſterday morning 140°. this morning 125°.

Tueſday, 9 *September*. This morning the curd came at its proper heat 80°. and the heat of the ſcalding whey was 142°.

The curd being thoroughly mixed and agitated among the whey, and having had a few minutes to ſubſide in,—the dairymaid began immediately to lade off the whey. This, however, is not the univerſal practice: in ſome dairies the curd is ſuffered to remain among the ſcalding ſtuff half an hour: thus (as has been obſerved) there are *ſhades of difference* in every ſtage of the proceſs.

Wedneſday, 24 *Sept*. This morning, the curdcame too tender; and the morning being cool; the ſcalding whey was heated to 161°.

and

and ſtood upon the curd near ten minutes: this changed it from a ſtate of jelly as to ſoftneſs, to the ſame tough hard maſs it is always left after ſcalding.

4. *Vatting.* The ſcalding liquor being moſtly laded off, a vat is placed on the cheeſe ladder, laid acroſs the tub, and the curd crumbled into it with the hands, ſcrupulouſly breaking every lump; ſqueezing out the whey as the handfuls are taken up; and again preſſing it with the hands in the vat; which is every now-and-then ſet on-edge to let the whey run off.

The vat being filled as full and firmly as the hand alone can fill it; and rounded up high in the middle; a cheeſe cloth is ſpread over it, and the curd turned out of the vat into the cloth: the vat waſhed or rather dipped in the whey; and the inverted maſs of curd with the cloth under it, returned into the vat. The angles, formed by the bottom of the vat, are pared off and crumbled upon the top, with which they are incorporated by partially breaking the ſurface, and rounded up in the middle as before; the cloth folded over and tucked in;

in; and the vat with its contents placed in the preſs. *

5. *Spare curd.* Preſerving the overflowings of the laſt vat of today's curd, to be mixed up with that of tomorrow, is a common practice in this country; where cheeſes, if they be intended for the factors, are obliged to be made of ſome certain ſize: the vats are all nearly of the ſame bigneſs; and cannot be proportioned to the curd, as they may when vats of various ſizes are made uſe of.

In the neighbourhood of Gloceſter, when the quantity of ſpare curd is conſiderable, as four or five pounds; it is frequently made into a ſmall cheeſe for the Gloceſter market; in which it may be ſold, in a recent ſtate (namely at three weeks to two months old,) for 2d.½ to 3d.½ a pound; according to its age:

* It is obſervable, that only one CHEESEBOARD is uſed, in the Gloceſterſhire dairies, let the number of vats be what they may. The bottoms of the vats being made ſmooth and even, they anſwer the purpoſe of cheeſeboards to each other——the uppermoſt only requiring a board. No "ſinking boards" are ever made uſe of here, as they are in other diſtricts; the vats being rounded up with curd in ſuch a manner, as, from experience it is known, will juſt fill them when ſufficiently preſſed.

age: three pence a pound is the ordinary price, for ſuch little two-meal cheeſes.

When the quantity of ſpare curd is ſmall, or where the making of little cheeſes is not practiſed, the whey is preſſed out and drained off as dry as may be, and the curd preſerved in different ways. In the upper vale I have ſeen it put into an earthen veſſel and covered with cold water. The next morning it is reſcalded thoroughly once or twice; broken as fine as poſſible; and either mixt evenly with the freſh curd; or, leſs eligibly, put into the middle of a cheeſe. *This*, however, is, with good reaſon, objected to by the factors. A harſh, crumbly, ill taſted ſeam is formed in the middle of the cheeſe; a diſagreeable circumſtance, which, in cutting a cheeſe, is too frequently met with. Mixing the ſtale curd more evenly among the freſh has an effect almoſt equally diſagreeable: the particles of ſtale curd ripen faſter than the reſt of the cheeſe; which is thereby rendered unſightly and ill flavored.

In a ſmall dairy it is impoſſible to make cheeſes ſufficiently *ſizeable* for the Glouceſterſhire factors, and at the ſame time avoid having, frequently, ſpare curd. But in a large dairy, where three or four cheeſes are made from one running, it might, by a proper number and aſſortment of vats, be generally avoided; and the cheeſes be at the ſame time made within ſize.

7. THE MANAGEMENT OF THE CHEESES. This requires to be ſubdivided agreeably to the different ſtages of management.

1. The management in the preſs.
2. The management while on the dairy ſhelves.
3. The operation of cleaning.
4. The management in the cheeſe chamber.

1. *The management while in the preſs.* Having ſtood ſome two or three hours in the preſs, the vat is taken out; the cloth pulled off and waſhed; the cheeſling turned into the ſame cloth and the ſame vat, (the cloth being ſpread under and folded over as before,) and replaced in the preſs.

In the evening, at five or ſix o'clock, it is taken out of the preſs again, and *ſalted* in this manner: the angles being pared off, if wanted, the cheeſling is placed on the inverted vat; and

and a handful of ſalt rubbed hard round its edge; leaving as much hanging to it as will ſtick. Another handful is ſtrewed on the upper ſide, and rubbed over it pretty hard; leaving as much upon the top as will hang on in turning. It is now turned into the bare vat, without a cloth; and, a ſimilar quantity of ſalt being rubbed on the other ſide, is again put into the preſs.

Next morning it is turned in the bare vat; in the evening the ſame; and, the ſucceeding morning, taken finally out of the preſs, and placed upon the dairy ſhelf.

Each cheeſe therefore ſtands forty eight hours in the preſs. At the ſecond or third, it is turned in the cloth: at the tenth, the cloth is taken off and the cheeſling ſalted. At the the twenty fourth, it is turned in the bare vat. At the thirty fourth, the ſame. And at the forty eighth finally taken out. *

2. *The*

* SAGE CHEESE. The method of making "green cheeſe", in this diſtrict, is the following. For a cheeſe of 10 or 12 lb. weight, about two handfuls of ſage and one of marigold leaves and parſley, are bruiſed and ſteeped one night

2. *The management on the dairy ſhelves.* Here the "young cheeſes" are turned every day, or every two or three days, according to the ſtate of the weather, or the fancy or judgement of the dairywoman. If the air be harſh and dry, the window and door are kept ſhut, as much as may be: if cloſe and moiſt, as much freſh air as poſſible is admitted.

3. *Cleaning.* Having remained about ten days in the dairy (more or leſs according to the ſpace of time between the "waſhings") they are cleaned; that is waſhed and ſcraped; in this manner: a large tub of cold whey being placed

night in milk. Next morning the greened milk is ſtrained off, and mixed with about one third of the whole quantity to be run. The green and the white milks are then run ſeparately; keeping the two curds apart until they be ready for vatting. The method of mixing them depends on the fancy of the maker. Some crumble the two together, mixing them evenly and intimately. Others break the green curd into irregular fragments, or cut it out in regular figures with tins for this purpoſe. In vatting it the fragments, or figures, are placed on the outſides. The bottom of the vat is firſt ſet with them; crumbling the white, or yellowed, curd among them. As the vat fills, others are placed at the edges; and the remainder buried fluſh with the top. The after-treatment is the ſame as that of "plain cheeſes."

placed on the dairy floor, the cheeſes are taken from the ſhelves and immerged in it; letting them lie perhaps, an hour or longer, until the rind become ſufficiently ſupple. They are then taken out, one by one, and ſcraped, with a common caſe-knife, ſomewhat blunt; guiding it judiciouſly with the thumb placed hard againſt its ſide, to prevent its injuring the yet tender rind: continuing to uſe it, on every ſide, until the cloth marks and every other roughneſs be done away; the edges, more particularly, being left with a poliſhed neatneſs. Having been rinced in the whey and wiped with a cloth, they are formed into an open pile (in the manner raw bricks are uſually piled) in the dairy window, or other airy place, to dry: and from thence are removed into the cheeſe chamber.

4. *The management in the cheeſe chamber.*—The FLOOR is generally PREPARED, by rubbing it with bean-tops, potatoe halm, or other green ſucculent herbage, until it appear of a black wet colour. If any dirt or roughneſs appear upon the boards, it is ſcraped off with a knife; and the floor ſwept clean with a hair broom. The cheeſes are then placed upon it,

regularly in rows: and kept turned, twice a week; their edges wiped hard with a cloth, once a week; and the floor cleaned, and rubbed with fresh herbs, once a fortnight.

The preparation of the floor is done with the intention of encouraging the blue coat to rise* To the same intent, the cheeses are not turned too frequently; for the longer they lie on one side without turning, the sooner the blue coat will rise. If, however, they be suffered to lie too long without turning, they are liable to stick to the floor, and thereby receive injury. If, by accident or otherwise, the coat come partially, it is scraped off.—This, however, seldom happens in a rich-soiled country, and all the care and labour requisite, in this stage, is to turn them twice a week; wipe their edges, once a week; and to prepare the floor, afresh, once a fortnight. If the cheese chamber be too small to admit of the whole being placed singly. The oldest are "doubled:" sometimes put "three or four double."

It is striking to see how well cheeses of this district bear handling at an early age: even at the

* See NORF: ECON:

the time of waſhing, the dairymaid will frequently ſet the cheeſe ſhe is ſcraping, on-edge upon another, lying flat on the table, without injury. At a month old, they may be thrown about as old cheeſes. Their rinds appear as tough as leather. This muſt be owing to the ſcalding. It cannot be owing to their poverty. They are evidently richer "fatter" than the new milk cheeſes of many diſtricts.

8. MARKETS for CHEESE in the upper vale. In large dairies, cheeſe is here ſold and delivered three times a year, namely in July;—again at Michaelmas; and finally in the ſpring. In ſmall dairies, only twice: about the latter end of September, and again in the ſpring.

It is bought principally by cheeſe factors, who live in or near the diſtrict. The ſame factor generally has the ſame dairy, year after year; frequently without ſeeing it, and, perhaps, without any bargain having been made, previous to its being ſent in. There is, indeed, a degree of confidence on the part of the buyer and ſeller, which we ſeldom meet with among country dealers. Millers and malſters buy by ſample, and generally take

take care to make a cloſe bargain, before the corn be ſent in.

In ſummer and early autumn, the factors will take them down to ſix weeks old; provided they be ſound firm marketable cheeſes; that is neither broken nor "hove:" a defect, which even the beſt dairywomen cannot always prevent. During winter, provided their coats be perforated to give the internal air an opportunity of eſcaping, the ſwoln cheeſes will generally go down, and, in the ſpring, become marketable.

The *conſumption* of twomeal cheeſe is chiefly, I believe, in the manufacturing diſtricts of this and other counties. Some of it goes to the London market; where it is probably ſold under the denomination of Warwickſhire cheeſe: and ſome is ſaid to go to foreign markets. The *ſize* moſtly "tens"—that is, ten to the hundred weight; or 11 to 12lb. each.

The *price* of twomeal cheeſe varies with that of newmilk cheeſe. At Barton fair, in 1783*, the "beſt making" ſold from 34s. (to

* Barton fair. A fair held annually on the 28th of September, in Barton-ſtreet, Gloceſter. It has long been the

(to the factors by the waggon load together) to 36s. (to families who bought by the hundredweight). "Two-meal," from 28s. to 29s. 6d. by the cwt. of 112lb. In 1788, "best making" 30s. down to 27s. "Two-meal" 25s. down to a guinea. Prices, which have not been heard of for many years past.

IV. Whey butter. It is the invariable practice of this district to set whey for cream. The lower class of People eat scarcely any other than whey butter. With due cleanliness and proper management, it may be made perfectly palatable; and, in every respect, preferable (while quite fresh) to the milk butter of some lean-soiled districts.

The whey is, here, generally set in one large tub: not parcelled out, thin, like milk. The

the principal cheese fair of the district. Formerly a principal part of the cheese, made in the two vales, was brought to this fair. At present, it is mostly bought up by factors previous to the fair. In 1783, there were about twenty waggon loads (besides a number of horse loads) exposed for sale in the fair. Some bought by factors; but principally, I believe, by the house-keepers, and the retail dealers of the neighbourhood. In 1788, the quantity in the market was much greater; about forty loads; cheese being then a drug.

The management of whey butter is ſimilar to that of milk butter. The price about two thirds of that of milk butter in the ſame market.

33.

S W I N E.

I. BREED. The tall, long, *white* breed, which was formerly, perhaps, the prevailing breed of the iſland, is here ſtill conſidered as the "true Glocesterſhire breed."—- They grow to a great ſize. At preſent, the *Berkſhire*, and a croſs between theſe two breeds, are the prevailing ſpecies. The Berkſhire are thought to be "hardier;" but are objected to, as being thicker-rinded, than the old white ſort. A mixture of *oriental* blood, is likewiſe diſcoverable in this diſtrict; but leſs, here, than in any other diſtrict I have obſerved in.

II. BREEDING,

II. Breeding, &c. Some are bred in the diſtrict: others *purchaſed* at Glouceſter market; probably the beſt ſwine-market in the kingdom. Seldom leſs than three or four hundred in an ordinary market. Moſt of them large grown hogs: many of them worth from fifty ſhillings to three pounds a head. Brought by dealers from Herefordſhire, Shropſhire, &c. Some of the ſmaller are bought by dairymen; the larger by dealers for the diſtilleries of Briſtol and London.

III. The food of store ſwine is principally whey, mixt with buttermilk, and given to them in a ſtale acidulated ſtate.—This, however, is not invariably obſerved: it is not unfrequently carried to them immediately from the dairy. While young, eſpecially when recently weaned, they have frequently the "ſweet whey" immediately from the cheeſe cowl; without having been previouſly ſet for butter.

IV. The proportion of swine to a given number of cows varies in the upper vale, where dairying and tillage are mixed in various proportions.—The ſubject is, indeed, in any caſe a vague one: the *number* depending on the

the *ſize*. The only general rule obſerved is, to endeavour to have always ſuch a *quantity* as the dairy will keep *well*: it being eſteemed bad management to overſtock a dairy farm with ſwine.

V. The materials of FATTING are whey, with beans cruſhed or whole; or with pea-beans; but ſeldom with peas alone.

VI. The MARKETS FOR BACON, are the manufactories of this and the neighbouring counties: the chief, I believe, is the "cloathing country,"—the woollen manufactory, in the Stroudwater diſtrict of this county.

LIST

LIST OF RATES.

VALE OF GLOCESTER.

BUILDING MATERIALS, &c.

OAK TIMBER 1s. to 20d. a foot.

Elm ———— 7d. to 10d. ——.

Clamp-burnt bricks 15 to 16s. a thousand

Slag, (copper drofs*) 5 or 6s. a ton, on the Kays.

Stone

* "SLAG." This, I underftand, is the *fcoria* thrown off by copper, in the procefs of fmelting. Until of late years, it was caft away as wafte, or ufed as a material of roads, only. Now, it is thrown, while hot, into moulds of different figures and dimenfions, and thus becomes an admirable building material. It is proof againft all feafons, in every fituation; confequently becomes an excellent material for foundations; and ftill more valuable for copings of fence walls: for which ufe it is fometimes caft of a fimi-elliptical form. It is alfo ufed as quoins, in brick buildings; in which cafe the blocks are run about nine inches fquare

Stone floors—(laid down) 4d. to 5d. a ſquare foot.

Lime—6d. to 8d. a buſhel.

Dimenſions of bricks 9—4½—2½ inches.

———— of plain-tiles 12 by 7½ inches.

Journeymen carpenter's wages 22d. a-day.

———— bricklayer's —— 22d. a-day.

BLACKSMITH's WORK.

Common heavy work 4d. a lb.

Shoing 5d.—Remove 1d.

TEAM LABOUR.

Hire of a team (waggon, five horſes, man and boy) 10s.

Price of plowing 6 to 9s. an acre.

——— harrowing 2 to 3s. an acre.

YEARLY WAGES.

Head man 7 to 9 or 10l.

Second man 5 to 7l.

Boy 2 to 4l.

Dairymaid 3 to 5l.

Undermaid 50s. to 3l.

DAY

ſquare, and eighteen inches long. It is of a dark copper colour; and has the appearance of a rich metal; but flies under the hammer as flint.

DAY WAGES.

In winter, 1s. a day and drink.

In hay harveſt, 14d. to 18d.—mowers not leſs than 18d. ſometimes more, with drink.

In corn harveſt, 1s. a day, or 30s. for the harveſt; with full board; or 2s. 6d. to 3s. a day, with drink, but no board.

Women, in autumn and ſpring, 6d. a day; but are ſeldom employed by the day in theſe ſeaſons; dreſſing graſslands being generally done by the job.

———, in hay harveſt, 6d. to 8d. a day, and drink.

———, in corn harveſt, 1s. a day, to thoſe who will work: but women in this country, as in moſt others, prefer "leaſing" to reaping. See York. Econ. i, 387.

TAKEN WORK.

Breaſt plowing a pea ſtubble, 6s. an acre.

Setting beans 16d. to 18d. a buſhel.

Hoing ——— about 6s. an acre.

Hoing wheat, 2s. to 4s. an acre.

Reaping wheat about 5s. an acre and drink.

Mowing barley; according to the crop.

Thrashing wheat, 3d. to 4d. a bushel (9½ gallons.)

——— barley, 2d. to 3d.

——— Beans about 1½d.

Mowing upgrounds 18d. and drink.

Mowing meadows 16d. to 18d.

Agistment price, in the hams, for one horse, *or* two cows, *or* six sheep, 25 to 30s. From Mayday to Michaelmas, or later. The hazard of floods is certainly an additional price: nevertheless, considering the superior quality of the land, it is low in the extreme.

PROVINCIALISMS

OF THE

VALE of GLOCESTER.

THE VERBAL PROVINCIALISMS of this diſtrict appear to be leſs numerous than thoſe of many other provinces. I have, however, had leſs converſation with mere provincialiſts, in this, than in other diſtricts I have reſided in. Beſides, it is obſervable, the lower claſs of people, here, are leſs communicative than they are, perhaps, in any other province: poſſeſſing a ſingular reſervedneſs toward ſtrangers; accompanied with a guardedneſs of expreſſion, bordering almoſt on duplicity: affording thoſe who are obſervant of men and manners, in the lower walks of life, ſubject for reflection.

WORDS, which relate immediately to RURAL AFFAIRS, I have endeavoured to collect.

 But

But I find they are few in number, compared with thofe collected in Norfolk and Yorkfhire on the fame fubject. Indeed, a lift of technical terms require a length of time, or the immediate fuperintendance of workmen, to render it complete.

Befide the deviations which are merely *verbal*, this quarter of the ifland affords, among others, one ftriking deviation in GRAMMAR;—in the ufe, or abufe, of the pronouns. The perfonal pronouns are feldom ufed in their accepted fenfe: the nominative and the accufative cafes being generally reverfed. Thus *her* is almoft invariably ufed for *fhe*;—as "her faid fo"—"her would do it": fometimes *he* for *fhe*;—as "he was bulled"—"he calved"; and almoft invariably for *it*;—all things inanimate being of the mafculine gender. Befide thefe and various other mifapplications (as *they* for *them*—*I* for *me*, *&c.*) an extra pronoun is here in ufe;—*ou:* a pronoun of the fingular number;—analogous with the plural *they*;—being applied either in a mafculine, a feminine, or a neuter fenfe. Thus "ou wull" expreffes either *he* will, *fhe* will, or *it* will.

This

This miſuſe of the pronouns is common to the weſtern counties of England and to Wales; a circumſtantial evidence, that the inhabitants of the weſtern ſide of the iſland are deſcended from one common origin. But in another ſtriking deviation; the PRONOUNCIATION of the CONSONANTS; their propenſities of ſpeech are ſo diametrically oppoſite; and ſo different from any tendency of utterance, obſervable in the reſt of the iſland; one might almoſt declare them deſcendants of two diſtinct colonies.

In Glouceſterſhire, Wiltſhire, Somerſetſhire &c, the ASPERATE conſonants are pronounced with VOCAL POSITIONS: thus *s* becomes *z*; *f*, *v*; *t*, *d*; *p*, *b* &c. On the contrary, in Wales, the conſonants, which, in the eſtabliſhed pronounciation, are accompanied with VOCAL POSITIONS, are there ASPERATED: hence *z* becomes *s*; *b*, *p*; *d*, *t* &c; —the mouth of the Severn being the boundary between theſe two remarkable propenſities of ſpeech.

In the PRONOUNCIATION of VOWELS this diſtrict, as Yorkſhire, has ſome *regular* deviation from the eſtabliſhed language; but differing, almoſt totally, from thoſe which are there obſervable: thus the *a* ſlender becomes *i* or *aoy*; as *hay*, "high" or "aoy"; *ſtay*, "ſty" or "zdoy"; *fair* "fire" or "voir"; *ſtare* "ſtire" or "zdoir" &c. The *e* long ſometimes becomes *eea*; as *beans*, "beeans": the *i* long, *ey* (the *e* ſhortened by the *y* conſonant); as *I*, "ey"; *ride*, "reyd": the *o* long changes here, as in the middle dialect of Yorkſhire, into *ooa*; as *home*, "hooam" or "wom";—the *u* long into *eeaw*; as *few*, "feeaw",—*dew*, "deeaw.

There are other deviations, both in grammar and pronounciation; as *be* is generally uſed for *is*; frequently *do* for *does*; and ſometimes *have* for *has*. But thoſe already mentioned are, I believe, the moſt noticeable, and in the moſt common uſe: I therefore, proceed to explain ſuch PROVINCIAL TERMS IN HUSBANDRY as have occurred to my knowledge in this diſtrict.

BLOWS

B.

BLOWS; bloſſoms of beans &c.

To BOLT; to truſs ſtraw.

BOLTING; a truſs of ſtraw.

BRAIDS; pronounced "brides;" ſee vol. ii. p. 283.

BROWN CROPS; pulſe; as beans, peas, &c.

BUTTER LEAVES; ſee p. 285.

C.

CALFSTAGES; ſee p. 225.

CARNATION GRASS; *aira cæſpitoſa*; haſſock or turfy air graſs; tuſſock graſs.

CHARLOCK; *ſinapis nigra*; the common muſtard, in the character of a weed.

CHEESE LADDER; ſee p. 268.

CLAYSTONE; a blue and white limeſtone, dug out of the ſubſoil of the vale.

COURT; yard; particularly the yards, in which cattle are penned in winter.

COWGROUND; cow paſture.

COWL; milk cooler; cheeſe-tub.

CRAZEY; the *ranunculus* or crowfoot tribe. See note p. 178.

CREAM SLICE; ſee p. 269.

CUB; a cattle crib.

D.

DAIRYHOUSE, or DEYHOUSE, pronounced DYE-HOUSE; (from *dey* an old word for milk, and *houſe*);—the milk houſe, or dairyroom.

DILL; *ervum hirſutum*; two-ſeeded tare; which has been cultivated (on the Cotſwold hills at leaſt) time immemorial! principally for hay.

E.

ELBOWS; the ſhoulder points of cattle.

EVERS (that is heavers); opening ſtiles. See p. 41.

EVERY YEAR's LAND; ſee p. 65.

F.

FALLOW FIELD; common field, which is occaſionally fallowed: in diſtinction to "every year's land."

FODDERING GROUND; ſee p. 230.

G.

GREEN; graſsland: "all green"—all graſs; no plowland.

GROUND; a graſsland incloſure, lying out of the way of floods; contradiſtinct from "meadow."

H

HACKLES; ſinglets of beans: ſee page 151.

To HAIN; to ſhut up graſsland from ſtock.

HAIRIF; *galium aparine*; cleavers.

HALLIER; ſee to HAUL.

HAM; a ſtinted common paſture for cows, &c.

To HAUL; to convey upon a waggon or cart, as hay, corn, or fuel: proper, but provincial: hence HALLIER; one who hauls for hire.

To HELM; to cut the ears from the ſtems of wheat, previous to thraſhing. The unthraſhed ſtraw being called "helm". Not a common practice here.

HIT; a plentiful crop of fruit

HOVE; ſwoln as cheeſes.

K.

KNOT; polled; hornleſs; ſpoken of ſheep and cattle.

L.

To LANDMEND; to adjuſt the ſurface, with a ſpade or ſhovel, after ſowing wheat; chopping the clods, lowering the protuberances, and filling up the hollows.

To LEASE (pronounced leeze) to glean : a term, which is common to the weſtern and ſouthern provinces.

LODE ; this ſeems to be an old word for *Ford* ; hence Wain Lode—-Upper Lode—-Lower Lode St. Mary de Lode &c.

LUG or LOG ; a land meaſure of ſix yards ; that is, a *rod*, *pole*, or *perch* of ſix yards ; a meaſure, by which ditching &c. is done: alſo the ſtick, with which the work is meaſured.

M.

MEADOW ; generally, common mowing ground, ſubject to be overflowed ; or any low flat graſs-land, which has not been plowed, and is uſually mown ; in contradiſtinction to "ground" and "ham."

MINTS ; mites.

MISKIN ; the common term for a dunghill ; or a heap of compoſt.

MOP ; a ſtatute, or hiring day for farmer's ſervants.

MOUNDS ; field fences of every kind.

N.

NAST ; foulneſs ; weeds in a fallow.

NESH ; —the common term, for tender or *waſhy*, as ſpoken of a cow or horſe.

O.

OXEY ; ox-like ; of mature age ; not "ſteeriſh."

PAILSTAKE ;

P.

PAILSTAKE ; fee p. 268.

PEASIPOUSE : peas and beans grown together as a crop.

POLTING LUG (that is, perhaps, *pelting rod*) a long flender rod ufed in beating apples &c. off the trees.

Q.

QUAR ; the common term for quarry.

R.

RAMMELY ; tall and rank ; as beans.

RUNNING ; rennet ; the coagulum ufed in cheefmaking.

S.

SEGS ; *carices* ; fedges.

To SET ; to lett, as land &c.

SETTING PIN ; dibble ; fee p. 144.

SH (without a vowel) gee ; in the horfe language.

SHARD ; a gap in a hedge ; the common term.

SHEPPECK : the ordinary name of a prong, or hay fork.

SIDDOW ; vulgarly ZIDDOW ; peas, which become foft by boiling, are faid to be " fiddow": a well founding term, which is much wanting in other diftricts. " Will you warrant them fiddow" ? is the ordinary queftion afked on buying peas for boiling.

SKEEL ; fee p. 269.

SLAG ; copper drofs. See p. 319.
STEERISH : fpoken of a young, raw, growing ox ; not "oxey."

T.

THREAVE ; twenty four boltings.
TUCKIN ; a fatchel ufed in fetting beans, fee 144.
TWO-MEAL CHEESE ; fee p. 287.

V.

VELL ; a calf's bag or ftomach, ufed in making "running."

W.

WAIN ; an ox cart, without fide rails.
WHITE CROPS ; corn : as wheat, barley &c.
WITHY ; *falix* ; the willow.
WUNT ; a mole ; hence
WUNT HILLOCKS ;—mole hills.

Y.

YAT or YATE ; a gate. This appears to have been once the univerfal name, and ftill remains the heraldic term, for a gate.

END OF THE FIRST VOLUME.

Lightning Source UK Ltd.
Milton Keynes UK
UKHW020705030219
336656UK00001B/2/P

9 781108 078801